More Praise for *Eat That Frog!*

"BEWARE: This book *will* have a profound impact on your working practices and the results you'll achieve. *Eat That Frog!* challenges your working practices, it explains the self-discipline needed to succeed, and [it] firmly gets to the root cause of why people procrastinate. Then it effortlessly explains how to boost your productivity once and for all."
—*Micro Business Hub*

"If you find procrastination to be a consistent problem in your life, *Eat That Frog!* offers a concise and valuable collection of tactics to try. The reasons for each person's procrastination are different, so it's good that Tracy's tactics are fairly diverse and attack many different avenues of procrastination."
—*The Simple Dollar*

"*Eat That Frog!* is my favourite book on productivity, and I often find myself rereading it in January to remind myself of the disciplines and practices I'd like to follow in the coming year. Each time I read the book, I find new nuggets of productivity gold."
—**Liz Gooster,** *Change for the Better*

"Everyone has a frog, and eating that frog is the best thing you can do to stop procrastinating. Procrastination is a time-killer, and Tracy has a way of making getting over that frog fun and exciting. Every chapter presents a new idea, tip, and technique that will help you overcome that inner laziness that keeps you on the couch at night instead of in the gym."
—*Peanut Press*

"*Eat That Frog!*, small in pages but huge in content, offers a cure for the curse of modern-day living: procrastination. Even though the medicine sounds painful (bush tucker trial kind of stuff), it isn't. Like you, I have read zillions of books—and most of the time I can't remember anything that I have just read. Not with this one. I'm eating frogs daily and feeling better for it! I can't recommend *Eat That Frog!* enough."
—**Corinna Richards,** *The Coaching Academy*

"This book gave me the kick in the pants I needed to organize my to-do lists, plan my days, become more productive, and get focused."
—**Beth Anne Schwamberger,** *Brilliant Business Moms*

"*Eat That Frog!* is the most accessible book on time management and personal productivity—I recommend you read this one before you learn any particular time management system. There are tons of exercises and techniques that you can implement right away, and that is what I like the most about the book—it gives you actionable steps so you can start right away."
—**Thanh Pham,** *Asian Efficiency*

"An impactful read. The 21 ways that [Tracy] shares are real game-changers, if you read with an eye towards self-improvement and an intention to make a change. I have benefited greatly from this book, and I highly recommend that you pick up your own copy today."
—**Chris Moore,** *Reflect on This*

"We strongly recommend this book to anyone who wants to manage her time well and also add value to herself in this competitive world."
—*The Journal of Applied Christian Leadership*

"I wasn't expecting all that much from the book initially, as the whole 'eating a frog' seemed like some new age nonsense that didn't really apply in real life. I couldn't have been more wrong. The best thing about this book is that it actually tells you what you should do. It doesn't just spout philosophy after philosophy about dreams and hope. It gives solid, practical advice that applies to pretty much every one—students, employees, stay-at-home moms, entrepreneurs, etc. Whether you're having time management issues or not, I'd recommend you pick up this book. You're sure to learn something useful from it."
—**Fab,** *Shocks and Shoes*

"This book distinguishes itself from others of the same type by laying out specific guidelines for developing the self-discipline that allows you to start and complete important tasks in sequence. Each of the 21 chapters offers clear instructions and practice exercises to help you determine if you are making the best use of your time at any given moment. You'll learn how to prepare yourself mentally and physically to tackle the task at hand, along with strategies for dividing it into manageable segments to keep you moving forward. You'll even find out what to tell yourself to do if you're having trouble getting started, or become distracted and need to get back on track."
—**Carnegie Library Business Librarians,** *Pittsburgh Post-Gazette*

Eat That
Frog!
for Students

Eat That Frog! for Students

22 Ways to Stop Procrastinating and Excel in School

Brian Tracy

with Anna Leinberger

BK®

Berrett–Koehler Publishers, Inc.

Berrett-Koehler Publishers, Inc.
1333 Broadway, Suite 1000, Oakland, CA 94612-1921
Tel: (510) 817-2277   Fax: (510) 817-2278   www.bkconnection.com

ORDERING INFORMATION
Quantity sales. Special discounts are available on quantity purchases by corporations, associations, and others. For details, contact the "Special Sales Department" at the Berrett-Koehler address above.
Individual sales. Berrett-Koehler publications are available through most bookstores. They can also be ordered directly from Berrett-Koehler: Tel: (800) 929-2929; Fax: (802) 864-7626; www.bkconnection.com.
Orders for college textbook/course adoption use. Please contact Berrett-Koehler: Tel: (800) 929-2929; Fax: (802) 864-7626.

Distributed to the U.S. trade and internationally by Penguin Random House Publisher Services.

Berrett-Koehler and the BK logo are registered trademarks of Berrett-Koehler Publishers, Inc.

Printed in the United States of America

Berrett-Koehler books are printed on long-lasting acid-free paper. When it is available, we choose paper that has been manufactured by environmentally responsible processes. These may include using trees grown in sustainable forests, incorporating recycled paper, minimizing chlorine in bleaching, or recycling the energy produced at the paper mill.

Library of Congress Cataloging-in-Publication Data
Names: Tracy, Brian, author. | Leinberger, Anna, author. | Tracy, Brian.
    Eat that frog!
Title: Eat that frog! for students : 22 ways to stop procrastinating and
    excel in school / Brian Tracy with Anna Leinberger.
Description: First edition. | Oakland, CA : Berrett-Koehler Publishers,
    Inc., [2020] | Includes bibliographical references and index.
Identifiers: LCCN 2020024900 (print) | LCCN 2020024901 (ebook) | ISBN
    9781523091256 (PAPERBACK) | ISBN 9781523091263 (ADOBE PDF) | ISBN
    9781523091270 (EPUB)
Subjects: LCSH: Procrastination. | Learning strategies. | Study skills.
Classification: LCC BF637.P76 T735 2020 (print) | LCC BF637.P76 (ebook) |
    DDC 371.30281--dc23
LC record available at https://lccn.loc.gov/2020024900
LC ebook record available at https://lccn.loc.gov/2020024901

FIRST EDITION
25 24 23 22 21 20   10 9 8 7 6 5 4 3 2 1

Design & Composition: Beverly Butterfield, Girl of the West Productions
Copyeditor: PeopleSpeak
Cover designer: Irene Morris Design

Contents

Preface

Thank you for picking up this book. I hope these ideas help you as much as they have helped me and thousands of others. In fact, I hope this book changes your life forever. Maybe a parent or teacher gave this to you, and if so, thank you for giving it a chance and making this commitment to your future!

It is an incredible time to be a student. Never before in history have there been so many resources available to you, so many opportunities, and so much potential. Once upon a time the only resource available to students was their teacher—and maybe a library if they were lucky. All students could do was learn from their teacher and research at the library, limited to whatever books happened to be in that collection.

Today, learning is limited only by how much or how little you choose to engage in the endeavor. Through any computer—your own, the library's, one you are given at school—you have access to educational resources your parents could only imagine. More than any time in history, you have the resources and ability to take control of your own learning.

Whether you are reading this book in high school, college, or even grad school, this is a turning point in your life. It is a time when your parents decide less and less what you must do, and you get to make more and more of those decisions. You are on the cusp of an extraordinary life—if you choose to seize the opportunity.

Start Here: There Will Never Be Enough Time

With all the demands on your time in school and outside school, you may already be overwhelmed by all your responsibilities. But the reality is there will never be enough time to do everything you need to do. This is true of your time as a student, and it will be even more true when you join the workforce. As if classes were not enough, you are swamped with everything else that comes along with being a student these days—a part-time job or an internship, sports, community service, the arts, or any other of the millions of activities and leadership opportunities clamoring for your attention.

Here's the reality: you can get control of your time and your life only by changing the way you think, work, and deal with the never-ending river of responsibilities that flows over you each day. You can take control of your tasks and activities only to the degree that you stop doing some things and start spending more time on the few activities that can really make a difference in your life.

I have studied time management for more than forty years. I have immersed myself in the works of Peter Drucker, Alec Mackenzie, Alan Lakein, Stephen Covey, and many, many others. I have read hundreds of books and thousands of articles on personal efficiency and effectiveness. This book is the result.

Each time I came across a good idea, I tried it out in my own work and personal life. If it worked, I incorporated it into my talks and seminars and taught it to others.

Galileo once said, "You cannot teach a man anything; you can only help him find it within himself."

Learning from Successful People

Simply put, some people are doing better than others because they do things differently and they do the right things right. Especially, successful, happy, prosperous people use their time far, far better than the average person.

I came from an unsuccessful background. Early in my life I developed deep feelings of inferiority and inadequacy. I had fallen into the mental trap of assuming that people who were doing better than me were actually better than me. What I learned was that this was not necessarily true. They were just doing things differently, and what they had learned to do, within reason, I could learn as well.

This was a revelation to me. I was both amazed and excited with this discovery. I still am. I realized that I could change my life and achieve almost any goal I could set if I just found out what others were doing in that area and then did it myself until I got the same results they were getting.

Within one year of starting in sales, I was a top salesman. A year later I was made a manager. Within three years, I became a vice president in charge of a ninety-five-person sales force in six countries. I was twenty-five years old.

A Simple Truth

Throughout my career, I have discovered and rediscovered a simple truth. The ability to concentrate single-mindedly on your most important task, to do it well and to finish it completely, is the key to great success, achievement, respect, status, and happiness in life. This key insight is the heart and soul of this book.

This book is written to show you how to get ahead more rapidly in your studies. These pages contain the most powerful principles on personal effectiveness I have ever discovered.

These methods, techniques, and strategies are practical, proven, and fast acting. In the interest of time, I do not dwell on the various psychological or emotional explanations for procrastination or poor time management. There are no lengthy departures into theory or research. What you will learn are specific actions you can take immediately to get better, faster results in your work and to increase your happiness.

Every idea in this book is focused on increasing your overall levels of productivity, performance, and output and on making you more valuable in whatever you do.

You can apply these ideas to any task or activity you have. They are primarily focused on classes and academics but can also be used to manage your time practicing an instrument, motivate your performance on a sports team, manage your time in a part-time job, and manage your time overall, while balancing all the different well-rounded activities you engage in.

This book was written to be a resource to help you with whatever area of your life you are struggling in. Don't feel you need to read it cover to cover. After the first three chapters, you should look at the table of contents and go directly to whatever part or chapter seems most useful to you at any given moment. The resources in this book have been carefully organized to help you with what students in today's classrooms find to be their biggest challenges. In fact, some of the techniques can be useful in several domains, so while every chapter has something new to offer, you may see similar techniques suggested in multiple parts.

In all these areas, however, the one key to success is action. These principles work to bring about fast, predictable improvements in performance and results. The faster you learn and apply them, the faster you will move ahead in your education—guaranteed!

There will be no limit to what you can accomplish when you learn how to eat that frog!

Introduction

Eat That Frog

The technique that gives this book its title is one of the most powerful personal productivity techniques you will ever learn. In fact, if you use just this one tactic every day for the rest of your life, you will increase your productivity output by a factor of ten. This one technique alone will make reading this book pay dividends you can hardly imagine.

If you are like most students today, you are overwhelmed with too much to do and too little time. As you struggle to get caught up, new tasks and responsibilities just keep rolling in, like the waves of the ocean. College admissions are the most competitive they have ever been. Good grades are necessary but not sufficient. Leadership, volunteering, and showing a well-rounded set of interests and achievements are also necessary. If college is not your goal, working part-time in your chosen field while you are in school will keep you just as busy.

I'm going to let you know a fact of life that most people do not learn until they are much older. This fact is that you will never be able to do everything you have to do. You will never be able to participate in every opportunity or activity that comes your way.

Many of the extracurricular activities you do will have an important impact on your future. They can enhance your college applications, or they may be a way for you to gain experience in a chosen job while you are still in school. You have access to a huge number of possible activities, which is both wonderful and risky. These outside activities can be the source of overwhelm for many students, resulting in time commitments and priorities that compete with your academics.

These opportunities are wonderful because they provide you with places to show your leadership abilities. They offer the chance to come up with your own ideas, manage your own projects, excel by distinguishing yourself as an athlete, team captain, musician, editor of a school publication, or volunteer—the possibilities are endless.

But those endless possibilities also pose a risk. It is easy to get sucked in to saying yes to every activity, every club, every sport until you are drowning in commitments. It is important to be intentional about the activities you choose and to make sure you are getting the most out of every commitment you make. You must be strategic: each activity should be chosen with your larger, future focused goals in mind.

The Need to Be Selective

For this reason, and perhaps more than ever before, your ability to select your most important task at each moment, and then to get started on that task and to get it done both quickly and well, will probably have more of an impact on your success and your future than any other quality or skill you can develop.

An average person who develops the habit of setting clear priorities and getting important tasks completed quickly will run circles around a genius who talks a lot and makes wonderful plans but who gets very little done.

The Truth about Frogs

It has been said that if the first thing you do each morning is to eat a live frog, you can go through the day with the satisfaction of knowing that that is probably the worst thing that is going to happen to you all day long.

Your "frog" is your biggest, most important task, the one you are most likely to procrastinate on if you don't do something about it. It is also the one task that can have the greatest positive impact on your life and results at that moment.

Eventually, once you have a job, you will be able to tackle your frog first thing in the morning. However, as a student, you will usually be in class first thing in the morning and your time will be spoken for. You will have to eat your frogs according to your study schedule.

The first rule of frog eating is this: think of your frogs in the context of the time you have to study. On weekends, you can eat your frog first thing in the morning. At other times, always eat your frog at the beginning of any given study session. When you sit down to do your homework in the evening, always eat your frog first. Whenever you have a study hall, eat your frog first.

Which Frog Next?

The second rule of frog eating is this: if you have to eat two frogs, eat the ugliest one first.

This is another way of saying that if you have two important tasks before you, start with the biggest, hardest, and most important task first. Discipline yourself to begin immediately and then to persist until the task is complete before you go on to something else.

Think of this as a test. Treat it like a personal challenge. Resist the temptation to start with the easier task. Continually remind yourself that one of the most important decisions you make each day is what you will do immediately and what you will do later, if you do it at all.

The third rule of frog eating is this: if you have to eat a live frog at all, it doesn't pay to sit and look at it for very long.

The key to reaching high levels of performance and productivity is to develop the lifelong habit of tackling your major task first. You must develop the routine of "eating your frog" before you do anything else and without taking too much time to think about it.

Take Action Immediately

Successful, effective people are those who launch directly into their major tasks and then discipline themselves to work steadily and single-mindedly until those tasks are complete. It has been shown over and over that the quality of "action orientation" stands out as the most observable and consistent behavior that successful people have in common. Especially once you begin college, your ability to take action without a study hall or a parent's reminders will be the single most impactful factor in whether you succeed in your classes. It is important to begin building these habits as soon as possible. The earlier you start, the easier maintaining these habits will be throughout your life.

A Note on Technology

I began my life with very few advantages. In fact, I didn't even graduate high school! I eventually went on to earn my master of business administration, but my early experiences have been a powerful inspiration in my life. I have written seventy-five books, and it is important to me that each one be accessible to all people with a passion for improving themselves and their life.

Many well-funded school districts and private schools fully integrate technology into daily learning. However, in many schools across the nation, students barely have access to technology at all. It is possible that your school gives every student a laptop, but perhaps you instead do all your technology work with a computer from a laptop cart. No matter what level of access to technology you have, this book is for you.

With all this in mind, the tools in this book have been written to focus on the methodology and theory, not the manner of implementation. Two chapters deal explicitly with technology, but the majority of the tools presented here have been written such that anyone with just a pencil and piece of paper can utilize them to the fullest extent.

Nevertheless, digital tracking systems or apps can be excellent vehicles for implementing the methods in this book, and the number of tools available to students is enormous. Choosing the right tools and using them wisely is absolutely essential to increasing your productivity. The two chapters on technology offer guidance on this.

And no matter how you choose to implement the advice in this book, the most important goals remain that you take action immediately, complete 100 percent of every task you start, and take full responsibility for yourself and your aspirations. All the rest is detail.

Take Control of Your Education

Thanks to the accessibility of the internet, your education has never been more in your control. World-class educational resources can be at your fingertips in an instant. If you are struggling with math, you can log on to Khan Academy and listen to a lecture on the concept that is tripping you up. If you have questions your history textbook does not answer, you can probably find an interactive website built by the Smithsonian Institution or National Geographic Society that will help you fill in the gaps.

Many resources are available online, for free, that will help you understand more about yourself and how you learn. There are also resources that will help you learn and study more effectively. But it is up to you to find them and take advantage of them.

Up until this point in your education, your teachers and parents have been responsible for what you learn. Now it is up to you! You are in control of your own learning. You will have assignments and school curricula you are expected to complete, but there is no need to feel limited by this. You can go out and learn what you are most passionate about without asking anyone's permission!

Visualize Yourself as You Want to Be

There is a special way that you can accelerate your progress toward becoming the highly productive, effective, efficient person you want to be. It consists of your thinking continually about the rewards and benefits of being an action-oriented, fast-moving, and focused person. See yourself as the kind of person who gets projects and assignments done quickly and well on a consistent basis.

Your mental picture of yourself has a powerful effect on your behavior. Visualize yourself as the person you intend to be in the future. Your self-image, the way you see yourself on the inside, largely determines your performance on the outside. All improvements in your outer life begin with improvements on the inside, in your mental pictures.

You have a virtually unlimited ability to learn and develop new skills, habits, and abilities. When you train yourself, through repetition and practice, to overcome procrastination and get your most important tasks completed quickly, you will move onto the fast track in your life and studies and step on the accelerator of your potential.

Eat that frog!

PART ONE

The Three Pillars of Success

One aspect of success is more important than any other. As a student, you are perfectly poised to learn it early and make it the foundation for the rest of your life. Intentionally cultivating the mindset of a successful person is the number one most important thing you can do right now. Nothing will have as big an impact on your success as practicing and implementing the intentions, habits, and perspectives of successful people.

This book will teach you many tools to help you manage your time and prioritize. Putting even one of the tools in this book into practice will increase your productivity immensely. But if you cultivate the mindset of a successful person, every tool you use will have an exponentially greater impact.

I have spent my whole career studying the best, most successful people in the world, and I have discovered that a successful person's mindset is built on three pillars: a successful person has self-esteem, takes personal responsibility for his or her life and actions, and is relentlessly goal oriented. If you can adopt these three approaches to your studies, nothing can stop you from achieving everything you aspire to in life.

1

Self-Esteem

Everything that happens to you is a reflection of what you believe about yourself. We cannot out-perform our level of self-esteem. We cannot draw to ourselves more than we think we are worth.

IYANLA VANZANT

No mindset is more important to your life and potential for success than unshakable confidence and self-esteem. When you have courage and determination, you approach life and your dreams convinced of your ability to achieve anything you put your mind to. Imagine the possibilities for your life once you develop the ability to face your greatest challenges unafraid, secure in your belief that you can overcome any challenge and make the most of every opportunity that you seek out.

The great news is that this level of self-confidence and self-esteem is completely possible for you! The only thing standing in your way is fear. This chapter will help you conquer all kinds of fear, freeing you to accomplish almost anything you could dream of. The marvelous thing about self-esteem is that it is learnable. Some people start out life with high levels of self-esteem, but the vast majority of us (myself included!) start out life with low levels of confidence, feelings of inferiority, and self-doubt. But these are not unchangeable, and it is possible to learn self-esteem with practice. If you systematically practice the tools in this book, day by day, your levels of self-esteem will rise.

Where Fear Comes From

Fear and low self-confidence come from many places. Perhaps a teacher or a parent criticized you and you internalized a feeling of failure. Perhaps you compared yourself to someone else and could only see yourself as inferior. Unfortunately, even these smallest moments can grow in influence. You start to believe, at a very young age, that you are not good enough, not smart enough to be truly successful in life. These beliefs live deep in your subconscious and sabotage you without your even knowing it. But there is a way to change even these deeply hidden beliefs.

"No Limits" Visualization

I have given thousands of seminars to people all over the world. This is one of my favorite exercises to do with the people who attend. I ask them to think about the following question, using the full power of their imagination: "What would you dare to dream if you knew that you could not fail?" This is not an easy question to answer! We are so conditioned to think of possible limitations and negatives that it may take time to truly allow yourself to answer the question.

Ask yourself this question over and over for the next few days. Allow your answer to change and grow as the true implications of *"if you knew that you could not fail"* sink into your mind. After thinking about this for days or even weeks, you will start to see options and opportunities open up in front of you that you never thought possible—and you will start to see how they can become a reality.

The truth is that if you do not believe something is possible, it never will be. You must change what you believe to achieve greatness. Once you allow yourself to dream big, you begin to see that your dreams really are possible after all!

Internal before External

One immutable fact of the universe is what I call the Law of Concentration. It states, "Anything you think about constantly becomes your reality"; in other words, what you think about all the time is what you will become. When you think constantly about something, it becomes established deep in your subconscious mind, where it influences your behavior, your thoughts, your choices, and your actions. If you think constantly that you are not good enough, this thought process starts to exert power over you, becoming a self-fulfilling prophecy.

However, another law, called the Law of Becoming, states that we are never static and unchanging: we are all always *becoming*, or evolving and growing. Every moment you have the ability to influence what you are becoming. Since you can control your thoughts, you can control what you become. In changing your thoughts, you have the power to control your future.

Resolve today to fill your mind with thoughts of the confident, happy, successful person you want to become. As you think these thoughts, they will begin to exert their subtle influence on your actions. You will begin to act in ways that are consistent with this powerful vision of yourself. One day you will wake up and realize you have become the confident, successful person you visualized today.

Decide on Your Values

Sometimes even visualizing the confident you might seem like a challenge. This is normal! Values are a very powerful tool that can help you to build this vision of yourself. Confidence comes from purpose and values. When you identify your values, you give yourself a clear road map to follow. Whenever you are faced with a choice, think over your values and use them as your guide. When you do this, you will always be assured that you are acting with purpose. The more you act in accordance with your values, the more confident you will become.

Right now, take a moment to identify your most important values. Values are things that you want to be known for—what you want to stand for. They can be things such as "taking care of my family," "getting good grades in school," "always being willing to help," and "always being transparent and honest." If you are having trouble identifying your values, think about people you admire. Why do you admire them? What values and habits do they have that make you respect them? And what do you want people to say about you?

Your values must be absolute—things that you strive to never, ever compromise on. If you would compromise on something, it does not qualify as a value. Of course, no one is perfect, and at times you will struggle with sticking to your values. The important point is that you keep trying. Always return to these values and recommit to them and you will continue to make progress.

When you identify your values and continually choose to live in congruence with them, you will begin to feel a sense of purpose and pride that lifts you up. You will feel confidence and self-assurance like never before. The more you do this, the more powerful your self-esteem becomes.

Choose to Leave Your Comfort Zone

Now, while everything I've written about is possible, it isn't always going to be easy. Humans have a tendency to slip into a comfort zone—doing only those things that they feel are easy, predictable, and safe. The comfort zone is the enemy of success. It is impossible to achieve greatness while staying in your comfort zone.

Getting out of your comfort zone is, in fact, uncomfortable! All of us have a tendency to become so addicted to our comfort zones that we will try to recreate them even when something forces us out of them. The reality is, though, that you will never grow if you stay inside this framework.

The answer is to never stop striving. Never shy away from an opportunity to get out of your comfort zone. Embrace challenge, and even seek it out! When you find yourself tempted to make the comfortable choice, to do what you have always done, stop, take a deep breath, and make a different choice. See where that new choice might take you—you will never cease to be amazed at what you can achieve when you choose growth over complacency.

Always Choose to Take the Next Step

The ultimate secret of self-esteem is that it is not something you *have*: self-esteem is something you *do*. To experience high levels of self-esteem, you must always choose to take positive, constructive action to move yourself and your dreams forward. Choose the challenge. Choose the option that aligns with your values. Always take decisive, determined action. In this way, self-esteem works in a cycle of reciprocity: the more you do, the better you will feel about yourself—and the better you feel about yourself, the more you will be both inclined to do and capable of doing.

When you always choose to take the next step, to move yourself forward, you will develop a sense of self-confidence and self-esteem that will be obvious to everyone around you. You will move ever closer to your goals and dreams, and eventually you will become an unstoppable force, capable of doing anything and everything you set your mind to.

EAT THAT FROG!

1. Ask yourself what you would accomplish if you knew that failure was impossible and you were guaranteed to succeed. Write down your answer in complete detail. What does your life look like? How did your success change your life for the better? Be very specific!

2. Revisit your visualization after a week. What else can you add? What dreams can you add that are even bigger and bolder than what you wrote down last week? Remember, you cannot fail.

3. Write a list of your ten most treasured values. What do you want to be known and remembered for? Put this list somewhere you will see it every day.

2

Personal Responsibility

Man is condemned to be free . . . because
once thrown into the world, he is responsible
for everything he does.

JEAN-PAUL SARTRE

One skill will be more crucial to your success, both
in school and throughout your whole life, than anything
else you can learn. It is the foundation of all successful
people, and without it, achieving your goals and dreams
is simply impossible.

This critical skill is the ability to take complete responsibility for yourself at all times. As a high school or college student, you are facing one of the first major turning
points in your life. Until recently, your parents have had
control over most of your life. They decided what you
wore and ate, what you did, and where you went. They
made sure that you got to school on time, that you did
your school projects and homework, and that you got to
sports practice and music rehearsals.

But now you have reached the point in your life where
these decisions and many others have become your
responsibility. Your ability to embrace this responsibility, completely and absolutely, will determine your academic and personal success. Personal responsibility and

self-discipline are the key to greatness—and they are 100 percent in your power.

It's All Up to You

So far in your life, taking responsibility may have been presented to you in a negative light. Perhaps as a child your parents impressed upon you the necessity of taking responsibility for your actions when you did something you have since learned is wrong. You may have unpleasant associations with these moments, feeling that taking responsibility is equivalent to a punishment.

In reality, nothing could be further from the truth! Taking responsibility is one of the best things about growing up. From this point forward, you get to make every decision and determine for yourself every action you take. Your life and choices are now your responsibility and in your control. Isn't that wonderful?

Some things will always be out of your control. You cannot control things like the weather, the actions of other people, or even many of the requirements you will have to fulfill to graduate. Taking responsibility means refusing to get angry or resentful about things you cannot control. Instead, always focus on your own reactions. It is your *reactions* that are under your control. No matter what happens, you get to choose how you *respond* to every single thing that happens to you for the rest of your life.

For example, you may have to fulfill a set of requirements to graduate. You may dislike one or more of these requirements. However, if your reaction to the requirements is to ignore them or put very little effort into them, you will either fail to graduate or graduate with poor grades. If you instead react by taking complete responsibility for your performance in those classes, you will graduate with high marks and go on to great success.

The best way to deal with the anger and negative emotions you may feel when faced with a situation you cannot control is to replace the negative thoughts with positive ones. Neuroscientists have found that it is impossible to be angry when you accept full responsibility for yourself. Simply saying the phrase "I am responsible!" over and over to yourself will crowd out those negative thoughts. This will allow you to think positively about what you choose to do.

Try thinking "I am responsible!" right now. If you internalize this philosophy, there is almost nothing that will be out of your reach.

Taking Control of Your Education

As a young person reading this book, you are living in an unprecedented era of education in human history. The last fifteen years have seen the landscape of education in the United States change drastically to reflect a holistic focus on all dimensions of life.

A 4.0 GPA (grade point average) alone is no longer sufficient to secure access to many of the upper echelons of higher education. Volunteer experience, internships, musical or artistic endeavors, club and activity participation, student leadership, sports, and a myriad of other activities are all but required for admission to colleges, internships, and jobs. Trying to fit all these activities into your schedule can be overwhelming but also exciting. Remember—it's all in your control!

You are responsible for what activities you choose, and you are responsible for how you manage your time. You may not want to tackle a certain challenge, or you may be so excited that you try to take advantage of every activity or opportunity presented to you. But no matter what you choose, remember that *you* are the one who gets to do the choosing.

Choosing how much time you spend on your classes and homework, how many activities you participate in, and when you work on each individual task will be your first experience with prioritization. You must learn to assess your deadlines, goals, and commitments and create a strategy that will ensure your success in everything you attempt. The chapters in this book will give you many tools for doing just that.

Refuse to Blame Other People

An unfortunate consequence of having our parents make all our decisions for us is that many people grow up feeling that if something goes wrong in their lives, someone else is responsible. But once you reach a certain age, this just isn't true anymore. This shift happens in young adulthood, when you are in high school and college. This is a critical turning point.

The temptation to blame external factors is a strong one, especially since it is very common. You will witness many people around you—your peers and even adults in your life—engaging in this mindset. This is because blaming other people is much easier than taking full responsibility for ourselves. It is easy to think that someone else is the bad guy, and you are the victim.

Thinking this way inevitably leads to a spiral of excuses, guilt, and then more blame. When you are blaming others for your situation, it is impossible to take personal responsibility, and you lose all control over yourself and your choices. This is why blaming others will prevent you from achieving any dream you have for yourself or your future.

Resolve today to refuse to blame other people or external circumstances for your actions.

Taking Control of Your Own Life

Taking responsibility is hard and requires immense self-discipline, but it results in incredibly powerful rewards. There is a direct relationship between the amount of responsibility you accept and the amount of control you have over your life. The more you accept responsibility, the greater sense of control you will feel.

There is also a direct relationship between control and happiness. The more control you feel over your own life, the more positive and content you become. Personal responsibility is the fastest and most direct pathway to leading a life of fulfillment, contentment, and happiness.

Remember to say to yourself "I am responsible!" and repeat the thought over and over if you need to. Filling your head with this thought will help you overcome negative emotions that make it hard to make progress toward your goals. If you accept 100 percent responsibility 100 percent of the time and commit to using the tools in this book, you will become unstoppable!

EAT THAT FROG!

1. Think of a situation in your life right now that makes you feel frustrated and powerless. Say, "I am responsible!" to yourself at least five times. How do you feel?

2. Write down three ways that you can react to this situation that you have control over. Resolve to take action on these three things right away.

3. The next time you find yourself in this situation, use this exercise to reframe your circumstances and remind yourself that you are responsible and you have complete control over your own actions.

3
Goals

Perhaps when we find ourselves wanting everything,
it is because we are dangerously close to wanting
nothing.

SYLVIA PLATH

I am about to introduce you to a tactic that will change the whole course of your life if you implement it today. Self-esteem is a mindset, and personal responsibility is both a skill and a mindset. They lay the groundwork and foundation for success, but to succeed in life, you will need one tactic above all others.

Nothing will propel you toward success faster than the practice of having clear, written goals. Having written goals is like putting a turbocharger behind everything you set out to accomplish in life. They will allow you to get everything you want in a fraction of the amount of time it would take other people.

What Is a Goal?

If you were to ask a successful person what he or she thinks about all the time, the most likely answer you would get is "What I want!" Thousands of successful people have been asked this very question—and given this very answer.

The most basic definition of a goal is simply "something that you want." A marvelous thing happens when you think constantly about your goals—you begin to attract the resources that you need to complete that goal. When your goal is foremost in your mind all the time, you will begin to notice when you encounter anything that will help you achieve that goal. You will naturally tell the people around you about your goal, so when someone who has a resource you need hears you, that person may offer to help you.

Goals can be long-term or short-term—"a job that pays well" or "an A in my calculus class." However, there are a few things that make a goal more likely to succeed. The two most important qualities of a goal are that it be *concrete* and *written down*.

Your goals should not be vague and general, like "I want to succeed in my academics." If your goal is too general, it will be impossible for you to see how to take action on it, and without a specific metric, the goal will not be sufficiently motivating. Instead, it must be something specific, like the exact grade you want in a certain class or on a specific test. It could also be a piece of music that you want to learn for orchestra, the number of goals you want to score by the end of soccer season, or a personal time record you want to break for a running or swimming event.

How to Write Good Goals: The Three Ps

Goals work hand in hand with our natural human psychology. The more you think about your goals, the faster you will achieve them. This ability of your subconscious mind is immensely powerful, but to activate this power, your goals must be phrased in a specific way. The key to writing good goals is to use the Three P Formula: *present*, *positive*, and *personal*.

Goals should be written in the present tense—as though you have already accomplished them. So instead of writing "I want to get an A in English," you would write, "I have an A in English class" or "I can play Beethoven's Sonatina in F Major by memory."

Secondly, goals must always be stated positively—stating the positive outcome rather than the negative you are trying to avoid. So instead of saying "I will stop procrastinating," you would write, "I plan my days in advance and always complete my to-do list."

Finally, all goals need to be in the first person, using the pronoun "I," followed immediately by a verb. This is a powerful signal that tells the brain that it should start taking action *now*. Don't start a goal like this: "My goal is to understand how to write a proof for a geometry problem." Always write, "I can write an accurate and complete proof for a geometry problem."

Ten-Goal Exercise

There is a very simple exercise you can do that will start to build your faith in the power of goals. I have shared this exercise with hundreds of thousands of people all over the world, and for many years now, repeat attendees have lined up after my talks and workshops to tell me how well it worked for them.

Take a sheet of paper and write out ten goals you want to accomplish within the next six months, using the Three P Formula. Put it away and don't look at it again until six months have passed; then take it out and review it. In almost every case, people tell me that they have achieved at least eight out of their ten goals! When you achieve success after doing nothing more than this simple task, it will feel like magic, and you will start to believe in the power of writing down your goals.

Goals Must Be Reasonable

Writing down your goals and then systematically work-ing to achieve them is a powerful technique; however, it is essential that you specify a realistic and reasonable timeframe in which to complete them. For you to achieve any goal, you need to truly believe that it is possible.

I made a mistake early in my life when I set myself a goal to earn an amount that was ten times as much as I had ever earned. I made no progress toward this goal, and I eventually realized that the goal was not helping me. It was such a huge leap, my brain did not truly believe that it was possible. My subconscious mind rejected it, and as a result, the goal had no motivating power.

It is important to honestly assess your starting point when you begin to set goals for yourself. If your goal is to memorize a Mozart concerto but you have been playing the piano for only six months, you will have to specify a realistic timeframe for the goal. If you expect to achieve such an ambitious goal in an unrealistic timeframe, your brain will do what mine did, subconsciously reject the goal as unrealistic, and you will not make progress.

If you are struggling with grades and your goal is "I have straight As in all my classes," you will want to look at your current grades and consider some intermediary steps. For example, if you currently take five classes and you have three Bs, one C, and one A, you might set escalating goals for the next three terms. By the end of your current term you might say, "I have As in two classes and Bs in the other three"; by the end of the following term, "I have As in all but one class and a B+ in the other"; then, by the third term, "I have As in all my classes."

Act Your Way into Feeling

It has been proven over and over in psychology that it is our actions that determine our feelings, not our feelings that determine our actions. The potential in this one small fact is truly mind-blowing: we have control over how we feel. You can determine for yourself how you want to feel by acting in the way that someone who feels what you want to feel would act.

This is also good news for you whenever you start a new task or endeavor. As a beginner, you are likely to struggle and even fail when you start out. This is normal! You might not feel like the amazing, confident person you want to be and instead experience self-doubt and fear. There is a powerful technique you can use to combat this; it is called "acting as if."

When you act "as if" you were already who you aspire to be, you will start to feel "as if" you were that person. If you want to be at the top of your class academically, look at how the people who get straight As spend their time, and then spend your time the same way. If you want to excel as an athlete, look at how the top athletes of your age train, and train like they do. In no time at all, you will go from acting "as if" you were successful to being successful yourself.

Persist, No Matter What

Above all, an unfaltering persistence and commitment to your goals is the single quality that will guarantee that you eventually achieve your goals. You will undoubtedly experience setbacks, failure, and frustration as you work toward your goals. This is inevitable, and there is a reason it is said that "the master has failed more times than the beginner has tried."

Persistence is more important than genius, more important than resources, more important even than talent. It is your ability to persist in the face of failure—to try again, try a different approach, and above all, always keep going—that will lead you to succeed beyond your wildest dreams.

Once you have written goals, almost nothing can stop you from achieving them.

EAT THAT FROG!

1. Write down three goals you have for yourself right now. Don't worry about the format at first; just write down the three things that come to your mind immediately.

2. Revise your goals using the Three P Formula—make each goal *positive*, *present*, and *personal*.

3. Specify a reasonable timeframe for each goal you have written down. Then post your three goals next to your list of values from chapter 1. If you do no other exercise from this chapter, at least try this one!

PART TWO

Learning How to Structure Your Own Time

Whether you are reading this book in high school, college, or even graduate school, you will almost certainly be struggling with how to manage your own time. In high school you are learning this skill for the first time in your life. In college you have more freedom and less structure imposed by school or your family than ever before. And in graduate school, you will be straddling two worlds, learning more in your field as a student but also contributing to cutting-edge research as an emerging scholar yourself.

Each of these educational levels comes with its own challenges and increasingly minimal levels of external structure. This means that you will have to learn to impose your own structures and stick to them! The tools in part 2 will give you many different ideas and resources to learn how to manage your time on your own.

Resolve right now to choose at least two of these tools and try them out for the next week. Remember—taking action immediately and decisively is one of the most important skills you will need to be successful.

4
Set the Table

There is one quality which one must possess to win, and that is definiteness of purpose, the knowledge of what one wants and a burning desire to achieve it.
NAPOLEON HILL

Before you can determine your "frog" and get on with the job of eating it, you have to decide exactly what you want to achieve. You will always have multiple classes, homework assignments, long-term projects like papers and lab reports, and looming tests. It can be challenging to figure out the best thing to do and the best time to do it!

Clarity is perhaps the most important concept in personal productivity. The number one reason why some people get more work done faster is because they are absolutely clear about their goals and objectives, and they don't deviate from them. The greater clarity you have regarding what you want and the steps you will have to take to achieve it, the easier it will be for you to overcome procrastination, eat your frog, and complete the task before you.

A major reason for procrastination and lack of motivation is vagueness, confusion, and fuzzy-mindedness about what you are trying to do, in what order, and for what reason. You must avoid this common condition with all your strength by striving for ever-greater clarity in your major goals and tasks.

Build Your Road Map

We've already talked about the general guidelines for setting good goals. Now, I am going to introduce you to a more specific, powerful formula for setting and achieving goals. You can use it in school and for the rest of your life. It consists of seven simple steps. Any one of these steps can double and triple your productivity if you are not currently using it.

Step one: *Decide exactly what you want.* Either decide for yourself or sit down with a parent, teacher, or advisor and discuss your goals and objectives. Talk with the person until you are crystal clear about what is expected of you and which priorities will be most useful to your academic career. It is amazing how many people expend enormous effort, day after day, on low-value tasks because they have not had this critical discussion with someone who can help them determine what is most important.

One of the very worst uses of time is to do something very well that need not be done at all.

Stephen Covey says, "If the ladder is not leaning against the right wall, every step we take just gets us to the wrong place faster."

Step two: *Write it down.* Think on paper. When you write down a goal, you crystallize it and give it tangible form. You create something that you can touch and see. On the other hand, a goal or objective that is not in writing is merely a wish or a fantasy. It has no energy behind it. Unwritten goals lead to confusion, vagueness, misdirection, and numerous mistakes.

There are seemingly endless options today for digital goal tracking, and if these truly work for you, then by all means keep using them. However, if you find yourself constantly chasing and downloading the next promising app but never using it for more than a few weeks, it might be time to try some old-fashioned pen and paper. One of the benefits of writing things on paper is the possibility of putting it somewhere that you can see it all the time. If you have only captured your goals digitally, you will see them only when you open the app where you have them saved. A list written on paper is something you can place on your desk, so even when your next text message comes in or you have to open Duolingo to do your language homework, you will still be able to see your list of goals.

Step three: *Set a deadline on your goal; set subdeadlines if necessary.* Your teachers will determine the deadlines for most of your assignments. Meeting deadlines is an important skill to learn because once you graduate and join the workforce, you will have to set your own deadlines. A goal or decision without a deadline has no urgency. When you have a large number of tasks to balance, creating your own subdeadlines can help you stay on track to meet your teachers' deadlines. Without subdeadlines, you will naturally procrastinate and may end up being forced to stay up all night, scrambling to get your assignments done right before they are due.

Step four: *Think through each of your assignments and make a list of everything you can think of that you are going to have to do to complete them.* As you think of new tasks, add them to your list. Keep building your list until it is complete. A list gives you a visual picture of the larger task or objective. It gives you a track to run on. It dramatically increases the likelihood that you will achieve your goal as you have defined it and on schedule.

Step five: *Organize the list into a plan.* Organize your list by priority and sequence. List all tasks in the order they need to be done. Take a few minutes to decide what you need to do first and what you can do later. Decide what has to be done before something else and what needs to be done afterward.

Even better, lay out your plan visually in the form of a series of boxes or circles on a sheet of paper, with lines and arrows showing the relationship of each task to every other task (fig. 1). You'll be amazed at how much easier it is to achieve your goal when you break it down into individual tasks.

With a written goal and an organized plan of action, you will be far more productive and efficient than people who are carrying their goals around in their minds.

Step six: *Take action on your plan immediately.* Do something. Do anything. An average plan vigorously executed is far better than a brilliant plan on which nothing is

GOAL – I have completed my 4 page History paper by Oct. 15 - 3 weeks
    Week One: Begin research and complete outline
    Week Two: Write rough draft and give to peer review partner
    Week Three: Review peer feedback and revise, proofread, turn in

TASK LIST

- Decide topic and preliminary thesis
- Reread textbook section on my topic
- Look up 3+ sources of research for my topic
- Take notes on sources
- Write complete bibliography entry for every source right away as I use it (finish bibliography as I go!)
- Revisit preliminary thesis to make sure new research supports it, revise thesis as necessary
- Determine 3 facts or arguments that support the argument my thesis is making: these are the 3 supporting points for the essay
- Write intro/thesis paragraph, one paragraph per supporting point, and conclusion
- Spell check with computer and manually, looking for typos and homonyms
- Have peer review partner read and give comments
- Revise according to feedback
- Do one last proofread of paper and bibliography
- Turn paper in!

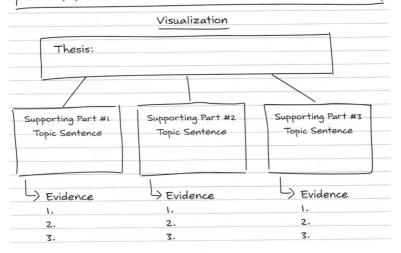

Visualization

Figure 1. Action plan

done. You have already done the hard work—your plan will tell you what to do first. For you to achieve any kind of success, execution is everything. Remember that you don't have to be perfect before you start; just start right away.

Step seven: *Resolve to do something every single day that moves you toward your major goal.* Build the activity into your daily schedule. Whatever it is, you must never miss a day. You may determine a specific number of hours and the time of day to do your homework. You may participate in a sport every day after school. You may decide to practice an instrument for thirty minutes every day. You may have to do all three of these things every day. It is critical to make sure that your plan is achievable and that you have time every day to dedicate to advancing your goals. If you find that there is not enough time, revisit your list of priorities and consider what you may need to cut.

Keep pushing forward. Once you start moving, keep moving. Don't stop. This decision, this discipline alone, can dramatically increase your speed of goal accomplishment and boost your personal productivity.

The Power of Written Goals

Think about your goals and review them daily. Every morning when you begin, take action on the most important task you can accomplish to achieve your most important goal at the moment.

Clear written goals have a wonderful effect on your thinking. They motivate you and galvanize you into action. They stimulate your creativity, release your energy, and help you overcome procrastination as much as any other factor.

Goals are the fuel in the furnace of achievement. The bigger your goals and the clearer they are, the more excited you become about achieving them. The more you think about your goals, the greater becomes your inner drive and your desire to accomplish them.

EAT THAT FROG!

1. Remember to always use the present tense, positive voice, and first-person singular so that your goals are immediately accepted by your subconscious mind. For example, you could write, "I have As in Chemistry on {date}," "I have an internship at X company on {date}," or "I have three college applications ready to submit on {date}."

2. Write a list of ten goals you have for your life right now. You can use the list of goals you made in chapter 3, or you can create a new list right now. Of these ten goals, select the one goal that, if you achieved it, would have the greatest positive impact on your life. Whatever that goal is, write it on a separate sheet of paper, set a deadline, make a plan, take action on your plan, and then do something every single day that moves you toward that goal. This exercise alone could change your life!

5 Plan Every Day in Advance

Planning is bringing the future into the present
so that you can do something about it now.

ALAN LAKEIN

You have heard the old question "How do you eat an elephant?" The answer is "One bite at a time!"

How do you eat your biggest, ugliest frog? The same way: you break it down into specific step-by-step activities and then you start on the first one. Learning to break down big assignments into manageable steps is a skill that will be as important to your future career as it is to your schoolwork. A great example of what this looks like is the history paper task list from chapter 4.

Your mind, your ability to think, plan, and decide, is your most powerful tool for overcoming procrastination and increasing your productivity. Your ability to set goals, make plans, and take action on them determines the course of your life. The very act of thinking and planning unlocks your mental powers, triggers your creativity, and increases your mental and physical energies.

Conversely, as Alec Mackenzie wrote, *"Taking action without thinking things through is a prime source of problems."*

Your ability to make good plans to guide your actions is a measure of your overall competence. The better the plan you have, the easier it is for you to overcome procrastination, to get started, to eat your frog, and then to keep going.

Increase Your Return on Energy

One of your top goals should be to get the highest possible return on your investment of your mental, emotional, and physical energy. The good news is that every minute spent in planning saves as many as ten minutes in execution. It takes only about ten to twelve minutes for you to plan your day, but this small investment of time will save you up to two hours (100 to 120 minutes) in wasted time and diffuse effort throughout the day.

You may have heard of the Six-P Formula. It says, "Proper Prior Planning Prevents Poor Performance."

When you consider how helpful planning can be in increasing your productivity and performance, it is amazing how few people practice it every single day. And planning is really quite simple to do. All you need is a piece of paper and a pen. The most sophisticated Outlook system, computer app, or time planner is based on the same principle. It is based on your sitting down and making a list of everything you have to do before you begin.

Two Extra Hours per Day

Always work from a list. When something new comes up, add it to the list before you do it. You can increase your productivity and output by 25 percent or more from the first day that you begin working consistently from a list.

Make your list the night before for the school day ahead. Move everything that you have not yet accomplished onto your list for the coming day, and then add everything that you have to do the next day. When you make your list the night before, your subconscious mind will work on your list all night long while you sleep. Often you will wake up with great ideas and insights that you can use to get your work done faster and better than you had initially thought.

The more time you take to make written lists of everything you have to do, in advance, the more effective and efficient you will be. Creating your list the night before will allow you to start your tasks without thinking or worrying about what to do first. There will be nothing to keep you from starting your work with no delay.

Different Lists for Different Purposes

You need different lists for different purposes. First, you should create a *master list* on which you write down everything you can think of that you want to do sometime in the future. This is the place where you capture every idea and every new task or responsibility that comes up. You can sort out the items later.

Second, you should have an *academic-term list* that spans your semester, quarter, trimester, or block. You should make this list at the beginning of every academic term. Some of your responsibilities will carry over from the master list—ongoing tasks such as musical instrument practice, a longer process like applying to colleges, community service, or goals related to your job. Other items on this list will change with your revolving classes and can be built from the syllabus you are given at the start of your term.

Third, you should have a *monthly list* that you make at the end of the month for the month ahead. This may contain items transferred from your master list and term list.

Fourth, you should have a *weekly list* where you plan your entire week in advance. This is a list that is under construction as you go through the current week.

This discipline of systematic time planning can be very helpful to you. Many people have told me that the habit of taking a couple of hours at the end of each week to plan the coming week has increased their productivity dramatically and changed their lives completely. This technique will work for you as well.

Finally, you should transfer items from your monthly and weekly lists onto your *daily list*. These are the specific activities that you are going to accomplish the following day.

As you work through the day, cross off the items on your list as you complete them. This activity gives you a visual picture of accomplishment. It generates a feeling of success and forward motion. Seeing yourself working progressively through your list motivates and energizes you. It raises your self-esteem and self-respect. Steady, visible progress propels you forward and helps you overcome procrastination.

Planning a Project

When you have a project of any kind—like labs for science class, papers for English or history, group projects, or even your college applications—begin by making a list of every step that you will have to complete to finish the project from beginning to end. Organize the steps by *priority*, what is most important, and *sequence*, which tasks you must complete in order. Lay out the project in front of you on paper or on a digital project planner so that you can see every step and task. Then go to work on one task at a time. You will be amazed at how much you get done in this way.

As you work through your lists, you will feel more and more effective and powerful. You will feel more in control of your life. You will be naturally motivated to do even more. You will think better and more creatively, and you will get more and better insights that enable you to do your assignments even faster.

As you work steadily through your lists, you will develop a sense of positive forward momentum that enables you to overcome procrastination. This feeling of progress gives you more energy and keeps you going throughout the day.

One of the most important rules of personal effectiveness is the 10/90 Rule. This rule says that the first 10 percent of time that you spend planning and organizing your work before you begin will save you as much as 90 percent of the time in getting the job done once you get started. You only have to try this rule once to prove it to yourself.

When you plan each day in advance, you will find it much easier to get going and to keep going. The work will go faster and smoother than ever before. You will feel more powerful and competent. You will get more done faster than you thought possible. Eventually, you will become *unstoppable*.

EAT THAT FROG!

1. Begin today to plan every day, week, month, and term in advance. Take a notepad or sheet of paper (or use your smartphone) and make a list of everything you have to do in the next twenty-four hours. Add to your list as new items come up. Make a list of all your projects, the big assignments you have to work through that have just one major final deadline.

2. Lay out all your major goals, projects, and tasks by *priority*, what is most important, and by *sequence*, what has to be done first, what comes second, and so forth. Start with the end in mind and work backward.

   Think on paper! Always work from a list. You'll be amazed at how much more productive you become and how much easier it is to eat your frog.

6

Study Strategically Using Long and Short Chunks of Time

Nothing can add more power to your life than concentrating all of your energies on a limited set of targets.

NIDO QUBEIN

School is a unique environment where you must learn a wide variety of subjects and skills. This is critical to your future success since the career you choose will require that you have many different types of skills and the flexibility to switch between them. You will need to know how to assess a situation and then find the best solution to the problem at hand.

In school, different skills require different methods of study. Some tasks are best accomplished in longer stretches of time, and some are better suited to shorter periods of focus. Learning how to tell which task is suited to which timeframe will vastly increase the effectiveness of your studying.

The Big Fish

Most of your large and important assignments will require longer chunks of unbroken time to complete. Your ability to carve out and use these blocks of high-value, highly productive time is central to your ability to make a significant contribution to your work and to your life. This sort of studying will have to be done on weekends or on evenings when you are able to dedicate significant time to your homework.

Successful students set aside chunks of time at least several hours long to work on major projects such as term papers, lab reports, experiments and research, or putting together college applications. These tasks require long, uninterrupted periods of time for you to make meaningful progress on them.

Schedule Blocks of Time

Many highly productive people schedule specific activities in preplanned time slots all day long. These people build their lives around accomplishing key tasks one at a time. As a result, they become more and more productive and eventually produce two times, three times, and five times as much as the average person.

When you have a weekend day or an evening with no externally imposed schedule, it is up to you to create your own schedule and then discipline yourself to stick to it. The key to the success of working in specific time segments is to plan your study time in advance and schedule a fixed time period for a particular activity or task. Chapter 19 has additional tactics for planning large chunks of study time in a manageable way.

Use a Time Planner

A time planner, broken down by day, hour, and minute and organized in advance, can be one of the most powerful personal productivity tools of all. It enables you to see where you can consolidate and create blocks of time for concentrated work. In the same way that your school gives you a schedule that says "9:00–9:50, 1st period, Math; 10:00–10:50, 2nd period, History," you can create your own predetermined schedule for your unstructured time (fig. 2).

Saturday		Sunday	
9:00 – 10:30	Reading for English	Morning	Family time
10:30 – 10:45	Break		
		12:30 – 2:00	Science lab report
10:45 – 12:15	Math problem set		
		2:00 – 5:00	Volunteer
12:15 – 2:00	Lunch with family		
2:00 – 3:00	Practice violin		
3:00	Free!		

Figure 2. Weekend schedule

During these scheduled working times, turn off your phone and other devices, eliminate all distractions, and work for the whole duration of your self-structured plan. One of the best work habits of all is to get up early and tackle some tasks in the morning for two to three hours. You can get three times as much work done on a weekend morning when your friends are not yet up and it is not yet time for familial obligations.

The Many Small Fish

Working on large projects is not the only kind of learning you will be doing in school. School at any level is also about learning and retaining information permanently. To learn a large amount of information, such as historical facts and mathematical formulas, your brain needs to review the new information repeatedly over weeks or months. Learning new skills, like how to solve a differential equation or how to play an instrument, also requires repetition in the form of practice.

During weekdays your class schedule may take up most of your time, in high school, but this will also be true in college to some extent. Your schedule during the day is largely planned out for you. The time you have for homework may be scattered throughout that schedule in the form of a forty-five minute study hall or an hour and a half between two college lectures.

You should reserve specific kinds of studying for these shorter periods. Studying for a test is an example of something that you will need to do over and over in short bursts of time. Learning new information takes our brains a long time and demands repetition. This is why cramming for a test the night before will leave you with almost no memory of what you learned months or even weeks later.

Instead of cramming, you can decide to study for an upcoming test during a study hall (fig. 3), but choose just enough material that you can focus on for forty-five minutes. Don't try to study all the material for the test or try to work on a term paper if you just have forty-five minutes. By the time you orient yourself and gather your thoughts to write, the period will be almost over.

Other good study hall tasks are reviewing flashcards for a foreign language class, reading a chapter of a book assigned for homework, and reviewing your notes using the learning methods you will see in chapter 15.

Study Halls

Mon: Math homework
Tues: Read 1 chapter of 1984
        Journal response assignment
Wed: History reading
Thurs: Math homework
Fri: Make Spanish flashcards for Unit 10

Figure 3. Study hall sample schedule

EAT THAT FROG!

1. Think continually of different ways that you can save, schedule, and consolidate large chunks of time. Use these times to work on important tasks with the most significant long-term consequences.

2. Make every minute count. Work steadily and continuously without diversion or distraction by planning and preparing your work in advance. Most of all, keep focused on the most important results for which you are responsible.

3. Choose carefully which tasks to do based on how much time you have. Choose memory reinforcement for short periods of time, and focus on long-term projects when you have several hours to work.

7

Apply the 80/20
Rule to Everything

We always have time enough, if we will
but use it aright.

JOHANN WOLFGANG VON GOETHE

The 80/20 Rule is one of the most helpful of all concepts of time and life management. It is also called the "Pareto Principle" after the Italian economist Vilfredo Pareto, who first wrote about it in 1895. Pareto noticed that people in his society seemed to divide naturally into what he called the "vital few," the top 20 percent in terms of money and influence, and the "trivial many," the bottom 80 percent.

He later discovered that virtually all economic activity was subject to this principle as well. For example, this principle says that 20 percent of your activities will account for 80 percent of your results. In business, 20 percent of customers will account for 80 percent of sales, 20 percent of products or services will account for 80 percent of profits, 20 percent of tasks will account for 80 percent of the value of any given employee, and so on. This means that if you have a list of ten items to do, two of those items will turn out to be worth much more than the other eight items put together.

It may seem challenging to implement the 80/20 Rule in your schoolwork. After all, you can't decide that a required class is of no use to you and just decide to drop it, and you can't decide that a few quizzes are less important and choose not to take them!

The 80/20 Rule is not about eliminating the bottom 80 percent—it is meant to help you allocate your time more effectively. You should be spending *more* of your time on the important 20 percent and *less* of your time on the bottom 80 percent.

Number of Tasks versus Importance of Tasks

Here is an interesting discovery. Each of ten tasks may take the same amount of time to accomplish. But one or two of those tasks will contribute five or ten times the value of any of the others.

Often, a single task can be worth more than all the other nine items put together. This task is invariably the *frog* that you should eat first.

Can you guess on which items the average person is most likely to procrastinate? The sad fact is that most people procrastinate on the top 10 or 20 percent of items that are the most valuable and important, the "vital few." They busy themselves instead with the least important 80 percent, the "trivial many" that contribute very little to results.

When you have a variety of assignments for a class, inevitably they will have a range of value. Homework assignments and regular quizzes will be worth fewer points, and major projects such as tests or term papers will account for much more of your grade.

The 80/20 Rule is a useful lens that can help you see which assignments need your focused attention and most of your time. This isn't to say that you should ignore that quiz! But you should make sure that you do not spend too much time on lower-value assignments and neglect studying for higher value tests and working on larger projects.

Focus on Activities, Not Accomplishments

You may see people who appear to be busy all day long but seem to accomplish very little. This is almost always because they are busy working on tasks that are of low value while they are procrastinating on the one or two activities that, if they completed them quickly and well, could make a real difference in their lives. For example, working on a complex lab report or research paper that is worth 30 percent of your grade is much more important than the daily journaling exercises that are collectively worth only 10 percent of your grade. It does not make sense to spend many hours on the small assignment if it means you will have less time to spend on your big assignment.

The most valuable tasks you can do each day are often the hardest and most complex. But the payoff and rewards for completing these tasks efficiently can be tremendous. For this reason, you must adamantly refuse to work on tasks in the bottom 80 percent while you still have tasks in the top 20 percent left to be done.

Before you begin work, always ask yourself, "Is this task in the top 20 percent of my activities or in the bottom 80 percent?"

Rule: Resist the temptation to clear up small things first.

The hardest part of any important task is getting started on it in the first place. Once you actually begin work on a valuable task, you will be naturally motivated to continue. A part of your mind loves to be busy working on significant tasks that can really make a difference. Your job is to feed this part of your mind continually.

Managing Your Many Activities

The 80/20 Rule can be especially helpful when you need to assess your extracurricular activities. When you think about your life goals, consider how each of your activities is helping you achieve them. While it is important to have a well-rounded selection of activities, it is also likely that only one or two of them is really moving you toward your goals.

If you find yourself falling behind in classes or feeling so much stress that it impacts your performance, take a hard look at all your activities. Which ones are the most important to your future? Which ones will have a direct, measurable impact on whether or not you achieve your goals?

Once you have identified the 20 percent of your responsibilities that will help you succeed, you will have a clear guideline to tell you how much time and effort to expend in every area of your life—and possibly an idea of which activities to bow out of.

Motivate Yourself

Just *thinking* about starting and finishing an important task motivates you and helps you overcome procrastination. The fact is, the time required to complete an important job is often the same as the time required to do an unimportant job. The difference is that you get a tremendous feeling of pride and satisfaction from completing something valuable and significant. However, when you complete a low-value task using the same amount of time and energy, you get little or no satisfaction.

Time management is really *life* management. It is managing the *sequence of events*. Time management is taking control over what you do next—and you are always free to choose the task that you will do next. Your ability to choose between the important and the unimportant is the key determinant of your success in life and work.

Effective, productive people discipline themselves to start on the most important task that is before them. They force themselves to eat that frog, whatever it is. As a result, they accomplish vastly more than the average person and consequently are much happier. This should be your way of working as well.

EAT THAT FROG!

1. Make a list of all the key goals, activities, projects, and responsibilities in your life today. Which of them are, or could be, in the top 10 or 20 percent of tasks that represent, or could represent, 80 or 90 percent of your results?

2. Resolve today that you are going to spend more of your time working in those few areas that can really make a difference in your life and academic success and spend less time on lower-value activities.

8

Slice and Dice the Task

The beginning of a habit is like an invisible thread, but every time we repeat the act we strengthen the strand, add to it another filament, until it becomes a great cable and binds us irrevocably, in thought and act.

ORISON SWETT MARDEN

A major reason for procrastinating on big, important tasks is that they appear so large and formidable when you first approach them.

Use the "Salami Slice" Method

One technique that you can use to cut a big task down to size is the "salami slice" method of getting work done. With this method, you lay out the task in detail, writing down every step in order, and then resolve to do just *one slice* of the job for the time being, like eating a roll of salami one slice at a time.

In fact, this is how your homework functions. Your teachers have the enormous task of imparting to you vast quantities of knowledge. Imagine if someone went to a physicist and said, "I need you to teach all of physics to a fifteen-year-old who has never studied it before." Intimidating, don't you think? But what does your teacher do? He or she breaks physics down into a set of principles that build on each other and teaches you one principle at a time. Each homework assignment you have is one slice of the larger academic discipline you are learning.

Psychologically, you will find it easier to do a single, small piece of a large project than to start on the whole assignment. Often, once you have started and completed a single part, you will feel like doing just one more slice. You will find yourself working through the assignment one part at a time, and before you know it, the whole thing will be completed.

Develop a Compulsion to Closure

An important point to remember is that you have deep within you an "urge to completion," or what is often referred to as a "compulsion to closure." This means that you actually feel happier and more powerful when you start and complete a task of any kind. You satisfy a deep subconscious need to bring finality to an assignment or project. This sense of completion or closure motivates you to start the next task or project and then to persist toward final completion. This act of completion triggers the release of endorphins, the neurological chemicals that help you cope with stress or pain. When released, they result in a pleasant feeling of energy and mild euphoria.

The bigger the task you start and complete, the better and more elated you feel. The bigger the frog you eat, the greater the surge of personal power and energy you experience.

When you start and finish a small piece of a task, you feel motivated to start and finish another part, then another, and so on. Each small step forward energizes you. You soon develop an inner drive that motivates you to carry through to completion.

"Swiss Cheese" Your Tasks

Another technique you can use is called the "Swiss cheese" method of working. You use this technique to get yourself into gear by resolving to punch a hole in the task, like a hole in a block of Swiss cheese. Instead of preslicing the task, as in the salami method, you just start working on whatever part of the task you can do immediately.

You "Swiss cheese" a task when you resolve to work for a specific time period on it. This may be as little as five or ten minutes, after which you will stop and do something else. You will take just one bite of your frog and then rest or do something else.

The power of this method is similar to that of the salami slice method. Once you start working, you develop a sense of forward momentum and a feeling of accomplishment. You become energized and enthusiastic. You feel yourself internally motivated and propelled to keep going until the task is complete.

You should try the salami slice or the Swiss cheese method on any task that seems overwhelming when you approach it for the first time. You will be amazed at how helpful each technique is in overcoming procrastination.

I have several friends who have become bestselling authors by simply resolving to write one page or even one paragraph per day until their book was completed. I know people who finished their dissertation three times faster than their peers simply by resolving not to let a single day pass without writing a full page of their thesis no matter what. And you can do the same.

EAT THAT FROG!

1. Put the "salami slice" or "Swiss cheese" technique into action immediately to get started on a large, complex, multitask assignment that you've been putting off.

2. Become action oriented. A common quality of high performers is that when they hear a good idea, they take action on it immediately. Don't delay. Try it today!

PART THREE

Studying Something You Are Not Interested in, and Still Doing Well

You will always have to do things in your life that don't engage your interest, but this can be particularly frustrating when you are still in school. Even if you know you want to be an engineer, you will still have to sit through years of history and English classes. You may be an aspiring musician, but you will still be required to go to gym and math class. And despite your feelings about the classes, you know that what you are learning is valuable. Motivating yourself to deeply engage in topics where you lack passion can be a challenge, but at the end of the year, your transcript will reflect the grades that you got in all your classes, not just the ones that you like!

The techniques and mindset tools in this part will help you strategically tackle all those subjects that are just not interesting to you. They cover mental frameworks to help you think about your work in new ways so you can generate genuine internal motivation. They also offer organization methods and tools that will help you complete tasks where you struggle to generate that motivation.

9
Consider the Consequences

Write injuries in dust, benefits in marble.
BENJAMIN FRANKLIN

The mark of the superior thinker is his or her ability to accurately predict the consequences of doing or not doing something. The potential consequences of any task or activity are the key determinants of how much effort you will need to expend on a particular assignment or class. This way of evaluating the significance of a task is how you determine what your next frog really is.

Dr. Edward Banfield of Harvard University, after more than fifty years of research, concluded that a "long time perspective" is the most accurate single predictor of upward social and economic mobility in America. A long time perspective turns out to be more important than family background, education, race, intelligence, connections, or virtually any other single factor in determining your success in life and at work.

Your attitude toward time, your "time horizon," has an enormous impact on your behavior and your choices. People who take a long-term view of their lives and careers always seem to make much better decisions about their time and activities than people who give very little thought to the future.

When you are required to study something that holds little to no interest for you, it is important to think about the potential consequences of not doing the work or not doing well in the class. It may be that your grade in this class will still be an important piece of a college or job application. Knowing this can drastically increase your motivation to work hard on something you do not enjoy.

Rule: Long-term thinking improves
short-term decision making.

Successful people have a clear *future orientation*. They think five, ten, and twenty years out into the future. They analyze their choices and behaviors in the present to make sure that what they are doing today is consistent with the long-term future that they desire.

As a student, you are at the point in your life where your long-term decisions can have an outsized impact on your future. Decisions you make about what classes to take and what opportunities to pursue have a huge potential to enable your future success.

Make Better Decisions about Time

Having a clear idea of what is really important to you in the long term makes it much easier for you to make better decisions about your priorities in the short term.

By definition, something that is important has long-term potential consequences. Something that is unimportant has few or no long-term potential consequences. Before starting on anything, you should always ask yourself, *"What are the potential consequences of doing or not doing this task?"*

Rule: Future intent influences and
often determines present actions.

The clearer you are about your future intentions, the greater influence that clarity will have on what you do in the moment. With a clear long-term vision, you are much more capable of evaluating an activity in the present to ensure that it is consistent with where you truly want to end up.

Think about the Long Term

Successful people are those who are willing to delay gratification and make sacrifices in the short term so that they can enjoy far greater rewards in the long term. Unsuccessful people, on the other hand, think more about short-term pleasure and immediate gratification while giving little thought to the long-term future. It may be more fun in the moment to neglect your math homework in favor of a concert, but the grade you receive in math class may have a significant impact on your future opportunities.

Denis Waitley, a motivational speaker, says, "Losers try to escape from their fears and drudgery with activities that are tension-relieving. Winners are motivated by their desires toward activities that are goal-achieving."

For example, reading ahead in your class assignments, meeting with your teachers during office hours or outside of class, and reading books on how to study and learn more effectively will all combine to have an enormous positive impact on your future. On the other hand, doing the minimum required to turn in an assignment, spending all your free time socializing, and opting out of all extracurricular opportunities may seem fun and enjoyable in the short term but inevitably leads to poor grades, underachievement, and frustration in the long term.

If a task or activity has large potential positive consequences, make it a top priority and get started on it immediately. If something can have large potential negative consequences if it is not done quickly and well, that becomes a top priority as well. Whatever your frog is, resolve to gulp it down first thing.

Motivation requires *motive*. The greater the potential positive impact that an action or behavior of yours can have on your life, once you define it clearly, the more motivated you will be to overcome procrastination and get it done quickly.

Keep yourself focused and forward moving by continually starting and completing those tasks that can make a major difference to your future.

The time is going to pass anyway. The only question is how you use it and where you are going to end up at the end of the weeks and months that pass. And where you end up is largely a matter of the amount of consideration you give to the likely consequences of your actions in the short term.

Thinking continually about the potential consequences of your choices, decisions, and behaviors is one of the very best ways to motivate yourself to undertake even the most unpleasant tasks.

Obey the Law of Forced Efficiency

The Law of Forced Efficiency says, "There is never enough time to do everything, but there is always enough time to do the most important thing." Put another way, you cannot eat every tadpole and frog in the pond, but you can eat the biggest and ugliest one, and that will be enough, at least for the time being.

When you're running out of time and know that the consequences of not completing a key task or project can be really serious, you always seem to find the time to get it done, often at the very last minute. You start early, you work late into the night, and you drive yourself to complete the work rather than face the unpleasantness that would follow if you didn't complete it by the deadline.

Rule: There will never be enough time
to do everything you have to do.

What this means is that you will never be caught up. However, you can always be on top of your most important responsibilities. The others will just have to wait.

Deadlines Are an Excuse

Many people say that they work better under the pressure of deadlines. Unfortunately, years of research indicate that this is seldom true.[1]

Under the pressure of deadlines, often self-created through procrastination, people suffer greater stress, make more mistakes, and have to redo more tasks than under any other conditions. It may feel gratifying to type your assignment at the last minute, all in one sitting, but the quality of your work will certainly be lower. Sometimes a job actually takes much longer to complete when people rush to get it done at the last minute and then have to redo it.

It is much better to plan your time carefully in advance and then build in a sizable buffer to compensate for unexpected delays and diversions. However much time you think an assignment will take, add another 20 percent or more as insurance. Plan to finish your assignments a few days before they are actually due—make a game of getting them done well in advance of the deadline. Try starting your assignments—even the long-term ones—the day or day after they are assigned. You will be amazed at how much more relaxed you are and how much better a job you do when you are on top of your most important tasks.

Two Questions for Maximum Productivity

You can use two questions on a regular basis to keep yourself focused on completing your most important tasks on schedule. The first question is *"What are my highest-value activities?"* Put another way, what are the biggest frogs that you have to eat to make the greatest impact on your grades? In your family? To your life in general?

This is one of the most important questions you can ever ask and answer. What are your highest-value activities? First, think this through for yourself. Then, ask your advisor. Ask your parents and teachers. Ask your friends, choosing those who are in your grade or a few years ahead of you. Like focusing the lens of a camera, you must be crystal clear about your highest-value activities before you begin work.

The second question you can ask is *"What is the most valuable use of my time right now?"* In other words, "What is my biggest frog of all *at this moment?*"

This is the core question of time management. Answering this question correctly is the key to overcoming procrastination and becoming a highly productive person. Every hour of every day, one task represents the most valuable use of your time at that moment. Your job is to ask yourself this question, over and over again, and to always be focusing on the answer to it, whatever it is.

During school hours, your answer should always be to pay close attention in whatever class you happen to be in at the time. Focusing intently on class material as it is presented is as powerful as the 10/90 Rule. In the same way that planning can save you large amounts of time, so does paying attention in class. If you have absorbed the information as your teacher presents it to you, it will be that much easier to comprehend your homework, remember the material for the test, and synthesize your thoughts for a big assignment.

The more accurate your answers are to these two questions, the easier it will be for you to set clear priorities, to overcome procrastination, and to get started on that one activity that represents the most valuable use of your time.

EAT THAT FROG!

1. Review your list of tasks, activities, and projects regularly. Continually ask yourself, "Which one project or activity, if I did it in an excellent and timely fashion, would have the greatest positive consequences in my work or personal life?"

2. Determine the most important thing you could be doing every hour of every day and then discipline yourself to work continually on the most valuable use of your time. What is this for you right now?

   Whatever it is that can help you the most, set it as a goal, make a plan to achieve it, and go to work on your plan immediately. Remember the wonderful words of Goethe: *"Only engage, and the mind grows heated. Begin it, and the work will be completed."*

10

Take It One Mile Marker at a Time

Persons with comparatively moderate powers will accomplish much, if they apply themselves wholly and indefatigably to one thing at a time.

SAMUEL SMILES

There is an old saying that "by the yard it's hard; but inch by inch, anything's a cinch!"

When faced with a subject or task that you have very little interest in, one of the best ways to tackle it is to get your mind off the huge task and focus on a single action that you can take.

Lao-tzu wrote, "A journey of a thousand leagues begins with a single step." This is a great strategy for overcoming procrastination and getting more things done faster.

Crossing a Great Desert

Many years ago, driving an old Land Rover, I crossed the heart of the Sahara Desert, the Tanezrouft, deep in modern-day Algeria. By that time, the desert had been abandoned by the French for years, and the original refueling stations were empty and shuttered.

The desert was 500 miles across in a single stretch, without water, food, a blade of grass, or even a fly. It was totally flat, like a broad, yellow sand parking lot that stretched to the horizon in all directions.

More than 1,300 people had perished in the crossing of that stretch of the Sahara in previous years. Often, drifting sands had obliterated the track across the desert, and the travelers had gotten lost in the night, never to be found again alive.

To counter the lack of features in the terrain, the French had marked the track with black, fifty-five-gallon oil drums every five kilometers, which was exactly the distance to the horizon, formed by the curvature of the earth.

Because of this, in the daytime, we could always see two oil barrels—the one we had just passed and the one five kilometers ahead of it. And that was exactly what we needed to stay on course.

All we had to do was to steer for the next oil barrel. As a result, we were able to cross the biggest desert in the world by simply taking it "one oil barrel at a time."

Take It One Step at a Time

In the same way, you can accomplish even the least enjoyable tasks in your life by disciplining yourself to take it just one step at a time. Your job is to go as far as you can see. You will then be able to see far enough to go further.

To accomplish a great task, you must step out in faith and have complete confidence that your next step will soon become clear to you. Remember this wonderful advice: "Leap—and the net will appear!"

This technique might sound very similar to the salami slice method in chapter 8; however, there is one critical difference. The salami slice method is a time management technique; you preplan the whole project and know all the steps you will need to accomplish, but you do just one slice at a time. The mile marker technique is a motivational technique. It is useful for situations when you have a project so big, you don't yet know the full scope. Not knowing the whole project can be a powerful, invisible demotivator. With the mile marker technique, you can always make a start, even when you can't plan everything in advance.

Excellence in any endeavor is built by performing one task at a time, quickly and well, and then going on to the next task. Financial independence is achieved by saving a little money every single month, year after year. Health and fitness are accomplished by just eating a little less and exercising a little more, day after day and month after month.

You can overcome procrastination and accomplish extraordinary things by taking just the first step, getting started toward your goal, and then taking it one step, one oil barrel, at a time.

EAT THAT FROG!

1. Select any goal, task, or project in your life on which you have been procrastinating because you are unsure of how to accomplish the whole thing. Identify just the single next action that you can take right now. If you are stumped, you might benefit from asking for help—and make that your next task.

2. Then immediately take action on that task. Sometimes all you need to do to get started is to sit down and complete one item on the list. And then do one more, and so on. You will be amazed at what you eventually accomplish.

11

Motivate Yourself into Action

It is in the compelling zest of high adventure and of victory, and of creative action that man finds his supreme joys.

ANTOINE DE SAINT-EXUPÉRY

To perform at your best, you must become your own personal cheerleader. You must develop a routine of coaching yourself and encouraging yourself to play at the top of your game. This is especially true of tasks and requirements that you are not excited or passionate about.

Most of your emotions, positive or negative, are determined by how you talk to yourself on a minute-to-minute basis. It is not what happens to you but the way that you interpret the things that are happening to you that determines how you feel. Your version of events largely determines whether these events motivate or de-motivate you, whether they energize or de-energize you.

To keep yourself motivated, you must resolve to become a complete *optimist*. You must decide to respond positively to the words, actions, and reactions of the people and situations around you. You must refuse to let the unavoidable difficulties and setbacks of daily life affect your mood or emotions.

Dwelling on how unpleasant you find requirements to be will only make them harder to complete. Instead, you must discipline yourself to focus on the positive things that completing these requirements will bring to your life.

Control Your Inner Dialogue

Your level of self-esteem, how much you like and respect yourself, is central to your levels of motivation and persistence. You should talk to yourself positively all the time to boost your self-esteem. Say, "I like myself! I like myself!" over and over until you begin to believe it and behave like a person with a high-performance personality.

To keep yourself motivated and to overcome feelings of doubt or fear, continually tell yourself, "I can do it! I can do it!" When people ask you how you are, always tell them, "I feel terrific!"

No matter how you really feel at the moment or what is happening in your life, resolve to remain cheerful and upbeat. As Viktor Frankl, a Holocaust survivor and famous writer and philosopher, wrote in his bestselling book *Man's Search for Meaning*, "The last of the human freedoms [is] to choose one's attitude in any given set of circumstances."

Refuse to complain about your problems. Keep them to yourself. As speaker-humorist Ed Foreman says, "You should never share your problems with others because 80 percent of people don't care about them anyway, and the other 20 percent are kind of glad that you've got them in the first place."

Develop a Positive Mental Attitude

In Martin Seligman's twenty-two-year study at the University of Pennsylvania, summarized in his book *Learned Optimism*, he determined that optimism is the most important quality you can develop for personal and professional success and happiness. Optimistic people seem to be more effective in almost every area of life.

It turns out that optimists have four special behaviors, all learned through practice and repetition. First, optimists *look for the good* in every situation. No matter what goes wrong, they always look for something good or beneficial. And not surprisingly, they always seem to find it.

Second, optimists always *seek the valuable lesson in every setback or difficulty*. They believe that "difficulties come not to obstruct but to instruct." They believe that each setback or obstacle contains a valuable lesson they can learn and grow from, and they are determined to find it.

Third, optimists always *look for the solution to every problem*. Instead of blaming or complaining when things go wrong, they become action oriented. They ask questions like "What's the solution? What can we do now? What's the next step?"

Fourth, optimists *think and talk continually about their goals*. They think about what they want and how to get it. They think and talk about the future and where they are going rather than the past and where they came from. They are always looking forward rather than backward.

When you continually visualize your goals and ideals and talk to yourself in a positive way, you feel more focused and energized. You feel more confident and cre-ative. You experience a greater sense of control and per-sonal power.

Even when you must complete a task that you don't enjoy or see much value in, an optimistic attitude will provide the motivation to propel you through the neces-sary tasks and assignments.

EAT THAT FROG!

1. Control your thoughts. Remember, you become what you think about most of the time. Be sure that you are thinking and talking about the things you want rather than the things you don't want.

2. Keep your mind positive by accepting complete respon-sibility for yourself and for everything that happens to you. Refuse to criticize others, complain, or blame others for anything. You may be required to take a class you don't like, but how you react to this requirement is up to you. You will still be held responsible for your homework, your grades, and your progress. Resolve to make progress rather than excuses. Actively search for what might be of value to you personally, even if that value is not central to the material.

12

Single Handle Every Task

Herein lies the secret of true power. Learn, by constant practice, how to husband your resources, and to concentrate them at any given moment upon a given point.

JAMES ALLEN

Eat that frog! Every bit of planning, prioritizing, and organizing comes down to this simple concept.

Every great achievement of humankind has been preceded by a long period of hard, concentrated work until the job was done. Your ability to select your most important task, to begin it, and then to concentrate on it single-mindedly until it is complete is the key to high levels of performance and personal productivity.

The less desirable the task is, the faster you should resolve to get it done. Single handling is hands down the fastest way to complete anything you set out to do. If you can single handle all the assignments you are not looking forward to, you will be able to quickly get to the classes that you are excited about.

Once You Get Going, Keep Going

Single handling requires that once you begin, you keep working at the task without diversion or distraction until the job is 100 percent complete. You keep urging yourself onward by repeating the words "Back to work!" over and over whenever you are tempted to stop or do something else.

By concentrating single-mindedly on your most important task, you can reduce the time required to complete it by 50 percent or more.

It has been estimated that the tendency to start and stop a task—to pick it up, put it down, and come back to it—can increase the time necessary to complete the task by as much as 500 percent. Each time you return to the task, you have to familiarize yourself with where you were when you stopped and what you still have to do. You have to overcome inertia and get yourself going again. You have to develop momentum and get into a productive work rhythm.

But when you prepare thoroughly and then begin, refusing to stop or turn aside until the job is done, you develop energy, enthusiasm, and motivation—even for a task you don't want to be doing. You get better and better and more productive. You work faster and more effectively.

Don't Waste Time

The truth is that once you have decided on your number one task, anything you do other than that is a relative waste of time. Any other activity is just not as valuable or as important as this one, based on your own priorities, even if this task is not one you would choose for yourself.

The more you discipline yourself to working nonstop on a single task, the more you progress along the "efficiency curve." You get more and more high-quality work done in less and less time.

Each time you stop working, however, you break this cycle and move back along the curve to where every part of the task is more difficult and time-consuming.

Self-Discipline Is the Key

Elbert Hubbard defined self-discipline as "the ability to make yourself do what you should do, when you should do it, whether you feel like it or not."

In the final analysis, success in any area requires tons of discipline. Self-discipline, self-mastery, and self-control are the basic building blocks of both character and high performance.

Starting a high-priority task and persisting with that task until it is 100 percent complete is the true test of your character, your willpower, and your resolve. Persistence is actually self-discipline in action. The good news is that the more you discipline yourself to persist on a major task, the more you like and respect yourself, and the higher your self-esteem will be. And the more you like and respect yourself, the easier it is for you to discipline yourself to persist even more.

By focusing clearly on your most valuable task and concentrating single-mindedly until it is 100 percent complete, you actually shape and mold your own character. You become a superior person.

You feel stronger, more competent, more confident, and happier. You feel more powerful and productive.

You eventually feel capable of setting and achieving any goal. You become the master of your own destiny. You place yourself on an ascending spiral of personal effectiveness on which your future is absolutely guaranteed.

And the key to all of this is for you to determine the most valuable and important thing you could possibly do at every single moment and then *eat that frog!*

EAT THAT FROG!

1. Take action! Resolve today to select the most important task or project that you could complete and then launch into it immediately.

2. Once you start your most important task, discipline yourself to persevere without diversion or distraction until it is 100 percent complete. See it as a test to determine whether you are the kind of person who can make a decision to complete something and then carry it out. Once you begin, refuse to stop until the job is finished.

PART FOUR

The Pressure to Achieve

College admissions have never been more competitive than they are today. Grade inflation has skyrocketed, and the possibility of earning a 4.5 GPA when the scale officially goes up to only 4.0 is a reality of the world you are competing in.

You may also have to hold down a part-time job while in high school or college, which only intensifies the pressure. As a student today, you are expected to do more than study: you have to show leadership in a number of activities outside of your classes as well. But remember— you are the responsible one! You are the one who gets to choose how to tackle this enormous challenge. You get to choose how to react to these expectations.

Handling big challenges requires hard work and focus. The techniques in this part will teach you how to think like a top performer, work like a top performer, and make strategic choices that will act like the rocket fuel for your success.

13

Develop a Sense of Urgency

Do not wait; the time will never be "just right."
Start where you stand, and work with whatever tools
you may have at your command, and better tools will
be found as you go along.

NAPOLEON HILL

Perhaps the most outwardly identifiable quality of high-performing men and women is action orientation. They are in a hurry to get their key tasks completed.

Highly productive people take the time to think, plan, and set priorities. They then launch quickly and strongly toward their goals and objectives. They work steadily, smoothly, and continuously. When working with the massive pressure to achieve at the highest levels in school, developing this sense of urgency can be a powerful mindset shift that will propel you forward.

Getting into "Flow"

When you work on your most important tasks at a high and continuous level of activity, you can actually enter into an amazing mental state called "flow." Almost everyone has experienced this at some time. Really successful people are those who get themselves into this state far more often than the average person.

When you're in the state of flow, which is the highest human state of performance and productivity, something almost miraculous happens to your mind and emotions. You feel elated and clear. Everything you do seems effortless and accurate. You feel happy and energized. You experience a tremendous sense of calm and increased personal effectiveness.

Leveraging this sense of calm will do wonders for combatting your stress. When you achieve a state of flow, you are 100 percent focused on the assignment in front of you, not worried about all the other priorities clamoring for your attention.

In the state of flow, identified and talked about over the centuries, you actually function on a higher plane of clarity, creativity, and competence. You often come up with brilliant ideas and insights that enable you to move ahead even more rapidly.

Trigger High Performance in Yourself

One of the ways you can trigger this state of flow is by developing a *sense of urgency*. This is an inner drive and desire to get on with your work quickly and get it done fast. It is an impatience that motivates you to get going and to keep going. A sense of urgency feels very much like running a race against yourself.

You have probably already felt this sense of urgency when you were rushing to finish an assignment in time for a deadline. The great news is that you can generate this same sense of urgency on your own and use it to get ahead rather than just keep up.

With this ingrained sense of urgency, you develop a "bias for action." You take action rather than talking continually about what you are going to do. You focus on specific steps you can take immediately. You concentrate on the things you can do right now to get the results you want and achieve the goals you desire.

A fast tempo seems to go hand in hand with all great success. Developing this tempo requires that you start moving and keep moving at a steady rate. The faster you move, the more impelled you feel to do even more even faster. You enter "the zone."

Build Up a Sense of Momentum

When you regularly take continuous action toward your most important goals, you activate the Momentum Principle of Success. This principle says that although it may take tremendous amounts of energy to overcome inertia and get started initially, it then takes far less energy to keep going.

The good news is that the faster you move, the more energy you have. The faster you move, the more you get done and the more effective you feel. The faster you move, the more you learn. The faster you move, the more competent and capable you become at anything you try—be it homework, music, sports, or anything else you put your mind to.

The faster you work and the more you get done, the higher will be your levels of self-esteem, self-respect, and personal pride. You will feel in complete control of your life and your studies.

Do It Now!

One of the simplest and yet most powerful ways to get yourself started is to repeat the words "Do it now! Do it now! Do it now!" over and over to yourself.

If you feel yourself slowing down or becoming distracted by conversations or low-value activities, repeat to yourself the words "Back to work! Back to work! Back to work!" over and over.

Nothing will help you more in your future career than for you to get the reputation for being the kind of person who gets important work done quickly and well. This reputation will make you one of the most valuable and respected people in your future field. Learning how to motivate yourself into action as a student is a skill that will benefit you for the rest of your life. As a student, you have an invaluable opportunity to develop early, and it will catapult you to success over and over in your lifetime.

EAT THAT FROG!

1. Resolve today to develop a sense of urgency in everything you do. Select one area where you have a tendency to procrastinate, and make a decision to develop the habit of fast action in that area.

2. When you see an opportunity or a problem, take action on it immediately. When you are given a task or responsibility, take care of it quickly. Move rapidly in every important area of your life. You will be amazed at how much better you feel and how much more you get done.

14
Put the Pressure on Yourself

The first requisite for success is the ability to apply your physical and mental energies to one problem incessantly without growing weary.

THOMAS EDISON

The world is full of people who are waiting for someone to come along and motivate them to be the kind of people they wish they could be. The problem is that no one is coming to the rescue.

These people are waiting for a bus on a street where no buses pass. If they don't take charge of their lives and put the pressure on themselves, they can end up waiting forever. And that is what most people do.

Only about 2 percent of people can work entirely without supervision. We call these people "leaders." This is the kind of person you are meant to be and that you can be if you decide to be.

Chances are, if you are the sort of student to pick up and read this book, you are already putting pressure on yourself to do well. However, it can be challenging to distinguish between that and the pressure coming from parent expectations, school requirements, and peers.

Take this opportunity to put all that aside and think about *you* and what *you* really want. What is your objective? This is the goal that you should be aiming for. When you take full responsibility and ownership of your goals, putting the pressure on yourself can become energizing and exciting rather than stressful and demoralizing.

To reach your full potential, you must form the habit of putting the pressure on yourself and not waiting for someone else to come along and do it for you. You must choose your own frogs and then make yourself eat them in their order of importance.

Lead the Field

See yourself as a role model. Raise the bar on yourself. The standards you set for your own work and behavior should be higher than anyone else could set for you.

Make a game of starting a little earlier, working a little harder, practicing a little longer. Always look for ways to go the extra mile, to do more than the minimum requirements of any assignment.

Self-esteem as defined by psychologist Nathaniel Branden as "the reputation you have with yourself." You build up or pull down your reputation with yourself with everything you do or fail to do. The good news is that you feel better about yourself whenever you push yourself to do your best. You increase your self-esteem whenever you go beyond the point where the average person would normally quit.

Create Imaginary Deadlines

One of the best ways for you to overcome procrastination and get more things done faster is by working as though you had only one day to get your most important assignments done.

Imagine each day that you have just received an emergency message and that you will have to leave town tomorrow for a month. If you had to leave town for a month, what would you make absolutely sure that you got done before you left? Whatever your answer, go to work on that task right now.

Another way to put pressure on yourself is to imagine that you just received an all-expenses-paid vacation at a beautiful resort as a prize, but you will have to leave tomorrow morning on the vacation or it will be given to someone else. What would you be determined to finish before you left so that you could take that vacation? Whatever it is, start on that one task immediately.

You may not be able to complete all the homework that will be due if it has not been assigned yet, but if you know you have an English paper due at the end of the month, you could get a big head start on that project. If you are in college, you probably have a syllabus. You could consider doing all the reading assignments ahead of time. When you get closer to the date of the class discussion, it will take you much less time to refresh your mind on the reading, and you will have learned it much more thoroughly.

Successful people continually put the pressure on themselves to perform at high levels. Unsuccessful people have to be instructed and pressured by others.

By putting the pressure on yourself, you will accomplish more tasks better and faster than ever. You will become a high-performance, high-achieving personality. You will feel terrific about yourself, and bit by bit you will build the habit of rapid task completion that will then go on to serve you all the days of your life.

EAT THAT FROG!

1. Set deadlines and subdeadlines on every task and activity. Create your own "forcing system." Raise the bar on yourself and don't let yourself off the hook. Once you've set yourself a deadline, stick to it and even try to beat it.

2. Write out every step of a major project before you begin. Determine how many minutes and hours you will require to complete each phase. Then race against your own clock. Beat your own deadlines. Make it a game and resolve to win!

15
Learn How
to Learn

The only certain means of success is to render
more and better service than is expected of you,
no matter what your task may be.

OG MANDINO

Ever since the day you walked into a school for the
first time, your teachers have been doing two things:
they have been teaching you what you are supposed to
learn, of course, but they have also always been teaching
you *how* to learn. Learning how to learn is one of the
most important skills you are taught in school.

Nothing is worse than studying for hours and hours
only to feel as though you still don't get it. Improving
the efficiency with which you study is one of the most
powerful ways you can increase your productivity. If
you are better at learning itself, you will need to spend
less time slogging through assignments that you don't
understand.

A major reason for procrastination is a feeling of inadequacy, a lack of confidence, or an inability in a key
area of a task. Feeling weak or deficient in a single area
is enough to discourage you from starting an assignment at all. Conversely, the better you become at eating

a particular type of frog, the more likely you are to just plunge in and get it done.

If you continually improve the rate and efficiency of your learning, you will naturally and effortlessly build confidence. Instead of feeling inadequate, you will start to feel enthusiastic and have all the energy you need to dive right in.

Take Control of Your Learning

The great news is that you don't need to wait for your teachers to teach you how to learn—you can take the lead on improving your learning yourself! There are many resources available that you can acquire and use on your own. There are books, online courses, audiobooks, and free digital tools and even games that you can find online to improve your learning skills. A list of some of these resources is included in the "Learning Resources" section at the back of this book.

One powerful shift you can make right now to improve your learning is to stop focusing on what you are putting *into* your head and start focusing on what you can pull *out of* your head.[1] Your teachers usually try to get as much into your head as possible, but it is up to you to be able to get the information out of your head in time for a test.

One reason some students study a lot and still struggle is that they spend more of their time studying what they already know. They miss what it is they don't know, which is the thing they should actually be studying!

When you sit down to study, before you start, give yourself a minitest. Write down everything you remember from your last classroom lesson or the last homework assignment. See how much you remember. Then open your notes and compare what you remembered with what you wrote in your notes and study materials. Whatever you did *not* write down is what you should focus more on when you study.

Never Stop Learning

You can improve not only your learning itself but also key skills that are useful for every subject. Improving your learning and your key skills will also improve your time management. Even if you are getting As now, every year you will move up a grade and will be faced with more challenging material. There are many key skills that you will use no matter what level of education you are in.

The better you are at a key skill, the more motivated you are to launch into it. The better you are, the more energy and enthusiasm you have. When you know that you can do a job well, you find it easier to overcome procrastination and get the work done faster and better than under any other circumstances.

One additional exercise can make an enormous difference in your ability to do well on your tests and assignments: identify the skills that are most important to your academic improvement, and then make a plan to continually upgrade those skills. Some examples to get you started are how fast you read, how to take notes when you read through a text for the first time, how well you remember multiplication tables or algebraic formulas, and how you approach and organize your process for researching a paper.

Refuse to allow a weakness or a lack of ability in any area to hold you back. Everything is learnable. And what others have learned, you can learn as well. Even if you feel like your academic achievement thus far has not been stellar, you can pursue certain things that are in your control. You can seek out extra help from teachers, parents, or even friends. If your school has a learning support center or writing center, you can access extra instruction through it. You can also find resources on your own, without parents or teachers. Take advantage of the books on learning how to learn in the resources section of this book, and check out the free online learning tools also listed there.

The best news is that you can learn whatever skills you need to be more productive and more effective. You can become better at any subject—math, writing, history, physics, any subject at all. You can become better at doing research. You can become better at conducting chemistry labs. You can learn to play your instrument in front of others or improve your auditions. You can learn to write effectively and well. These are all skills you can acquire as soon as you decide to and make them a priority.

The more you learn, the more you can learn. Just as you can build your physical muscles through physical exercise, you can build your mental muscles with mental exercises. And there is no limit to how far or how fast you can advance except for the limits you place on your own imagination.

EAT THAT FROG!

1. Identify the key skills that can help you the most to achieve better and faster results. Determine the study skills that will have the biggest impact on your grades and achievement. Whatever they are, set a goal, make a plan, and begin developing and increasing your ability in those areas. Decide to be the very best at what you do!

2. Make it a habit to always test yourself on what you remember *before* doing your homework. Then make a point to study what you *didn't* remember even more carefully.

3. Review the learning resources in the back of this book. Resolve to try at least one of these books or tools to improve your ability to learn. Even books that are written for your teachers will have useful information in them that you can use to teach yourself.

16

Identify Your Key Constraints

Concentrate all your thoughts on the task at hand. The sun's rays do not burn until brought to a focus.

ALEXANDER GRAHAM BELL

Between where you are today and any goal or objective that you want to accomplish, there is one major constraint that must be overcome before you can achieve that major goal. Your job is to identify it clearly.

What is holding you back? What sets the speed at which you achieve your goals? What determines how fast you move from where you are to where you want to go? What stops you or holds you back from eating the frogs that can really make a difference? Why aren't you at your goal already?

These are some of the most important questions you will ever ask and answer on your way to achieving high levels of personal productivity and effectiveness. Whatever you have to do, there is always a limiting factor that determines how quickly and well you get it done. Your job is to study the task and identify the limiting factor or constraint within it. You must then focus all your energies on alleviating that single choke point.

Identify the Limiting Factor

In virtually every task, large or small, a single factor sets the speed at which you achieve the goal or complete the job. What is it? Concentrate your mental energies on that one key area. This can be the most productive use of your time and talents.

There are many types of constraints you might be facing: you might not have a quiet study space, you might be in the wrong level of a class, you may be in a classroom with thirty-five other students and find it challenging to get your questions answered, you may have chosen too many extracurriculars, you may have a side job that makes it hard to find enough study time, or something else. But the limiting factor is always there, and it is always your job to find it.

The accurate identification of the limiting factor in any process and the focus on that factor can usually bring about more progress in a shorter period than any other single activity. Even when your limiting factor seems insurmountable, there is almost always something you can do to improve your situation once you have identified it.

The 80/20 Rule Applied to Constraints

The 80/20 Rule also applies to the constraints in your life and in your work. This means that 80 percent of the constraints, the factors that are holding you back from achieving your goals, are *internal*. They are within yourself—within your own personal qualities, abilities, habits, disciplines, or competencies. This may sound daunting at first, but this is actually good news. If something is internal, it is 100 percent under your control, and you will be able to eliminate it.

Some constraints may seem external but actually have a dimension that is under your control. For example, you may be working on a group project where another student is not pulling his or her weight. The other student's behavior or contribution is not under your control, but your contribution to the project is. It may not be fair, but you can still work hard to make the project a success. The only thing that matters is what grade *you* take away from the project.

Only 20 percent of the limiting factors are *external* to you. Only 20 percent are on the outside in the form of time commitments, family responsibilities, and resources.

Your key constraint can be something small and not particularly obvious. You may have to make a list of every step in a process and examine every activity to determine exactly what is holding you back. It can be as small as a lack of comprehension in one tiny area. If you can identify that area, you will be able to ask your teacher for help on something extremely specific, and he or she will be able to help you much more effectively and quickly.

Look into your life honestly. Look at your parents, your teachers, and your friends to see if there is a way in which one or more of them might unintentionally be holding you back. While this is unlikely to be purposeful or malicious, they might inadvertently be doing something that is negatively impacting your studies. It is important when addressing these issues to do so with respect.

It may be something as innocent as a teacher thinking you are shy and not calling on you as much as other students or a parent whose evening activities disrupt your homework time. Remember that even though these constraints are external, you are still responsible for your actions and the actions you take to improve your situation. If others are not willing to change their actions to help you, it is still your responsibility to find another way to deal with whatever is holding you back.

Talk to your teacher after class to express interest and enthusiasm for participating in class discussions. Ask your parents if they would be willing to let you study in a quieter part of the house or agree on quiet hours so you will be able to focus. If your friends are texting you constantly, choose to turn off your phone while you are doing homework; or give your phone to a family member to help you resist the temptation to chat, text, and allow yourself to be distracted by social media.

Follow Your Internal Compass

Sometimes a single negative perception on the part of a friend or teacher can be slowing down your whole learning process. If someone's negative perception is holding you back, you may not be able to change the person's opinion, but you can decide for yourself whether his or her opinion is factual or valid. If you conclude that it is not, refuse to let that person's perception of you impact your perception of yourself.

This is particularly challenging if the situation involves a teacher's perception of you. It is important to consider feedback from your teachers since their job is to help you improve. And if they are giving you a grade, you will need to address their concerns with that in mind.

Here is a wonderful way to reframe criticism: negative feedback should be considered a gift. Even when it is inaccurate, you can always learn something from feedback—negative or positive. It is up to you to decide how to react to it, and what you choose to do about it is in your control.

However, we must remember that teachers are human beings who are doing their best, but they can't tell the future. If you have dreams of attending a particular college, but your college counselor is not supportive, look up the data yourself. The statistics on incoming classes are posted online. Decide for yourself whether your grades and test scores qualify you, and if they are not quite there yet, you have the power to work toward that goal. This book has given you the tools. If you dream of being a writer but your English teacher says you don't have talent, respectfully disagree, and whatever you do, never stop writing. You can improve in any area of your life. If you believe in yourself, take complete personal responsibility for your learning, and use specific goals to guide you, nothing can stop you.

Look into Yourself

Successful people always begin the analysis of constraints by asking the question, "What is it *in me* that is holding me back?" They accept complete responsibility for their lives and look to themselves for both the cause and cure of their problems. This is the most powerful approach you can take, since anything that is *in you* is also *in your power* to change.

This can be challenging to learn for the first time, and you must have the honesty to look deeply into yourself for the limiting factor or limiting skill that sets the speed at which you achieve your personal goals. Keep asking, "What sets the speed at which I get the results I want?"

Strive for Accuracy

The definition of the constraint determines the strategy that you use to alleviate it. The failure to identify the correct constraint, or the identification of the wrong constraint, can lead you in the wrong direction. You can end up solving the wrong problem.

A teacher I know told me about a student of hers who designed a science experiment for his chemistry lab but was consistently getting nonsense results. Before he redesigned the whole experiment, he chose to talk to his teacher about his progress. She was able to help him see that his data was good—he was just misreading it. Instead of spending twice as much time to start over, he just changed how he was reading the data.

Your teachers and even your peers are valuable resources for you when you are trying to identify constraints. Once you are in the professional world, you will be solving problems on your own, but for now, you have the incredible support of teachers who can help you assess your work.

They won't solve your problems for you, but they will be able to guide you so that you get better and better at doing it on your own.

Behind every constraint or choke point, once it is located and alleviated successfully, you will find another constraint or limiting factor. Whether you're trying to get all your homework finished or make it to soccer practice on time, there are always limiting factors and bottlenecks that set the speed of your progress. Your job is to find them and to focus your energies on alleviating them as quickly as possible.

Starting off your day with the removal of a key bottleneck or constraint fills you with energy and personal power. It propels you into following through and completing your work. Often, alleviating a key constraint or limiting factor is the most important frog you could eat at that moment.

EAT THAT FROG!

1. Identify your most important goal in life today. What is it? What one academic accomplishment, if you achieved it, would have the greatest positive effect on your life? What one career accomplishment would have the greatest positive impact on your life and future?

2. Determine the one constraint, internal or external, that sets the speed at which you accomplish this goal. Ask, "Why haven't I reached it already? What is it in me that is holding me back?" Whatever your answers, take action immediately. Do something. Do anything, but get started.

17
Focus on Key Result Areas

When every physical and mental resource is focused, one's power to solve a problem multiplies tremendously.

NORMAN VINCENT PEALE

Succeeding in high school or college can be broken down into about five key result areas, seldom more. These represent the results that you absolutely, positively have to get to maximize the value you gain from your education.

With so many activities and opportunities competing for your attention, it can be difficult to remember what should take precedence. With seemingly endless options for clubs, sports, arts, volunteering, and more, it is possible to lose sight of the most important goal in school: doing well in your classes.

The single most important key result area for any student is your academic classes. Grades and performance in your major classes should always be considered your most crucial responsibility. This is why you are in school, and how well you do will largely determine what opportunities you will have once you graduate.

Other key result areas for students might include relationships with your teachers, which will determine what recommendations you are able to ask for, your ability to manage your own schedule and complete assignments on time, the student leadership you show in activities outside of your classes, and the community responsibility you demonstrate through volunteer work and community engagement.

Give Yourself a Grade

As a student, it is usually your teachers who will be giving you grades on your work. In this context, it can be tempting to see the situation as one in which you have no control, but in reality, nothing could be further from the truth. One powerful way to realize your own power as a student is to give yourself a grade on every assignment you do before you turn it in. Make sure to do this before the due date! Be honest with yourself about how you have done. If your teacher has given you a grading rubric, sit down with your assignment, pretend you are the teacher, and evaluate your own work. At a minimum, make sure to look at the original instructions for the assignment. Where are you strong and where are you weak? Where have you done excellent work and where could you improve your work?

> **Rule:** Your *weakest* key result area sets the height at which you can use all your other skills and abilities.

This rule says that although you could be exceptional in four out of your five key result areas, poor performance in the fifth area will still hold you back and determine how much you achieve with all your other skills. This weakness will act as a drag on your effectiveness and be a constant source of friction and frustration.

You can also look at any individual assignment and determine the key result areas for that assignment. For example, research is one of the most important steps in any assignment, no matter what subject you are working with. If you are grading yourself on an assignment and you give yourself an A on your writing and an A on your thesis but a B on how well you supported the thesis and a C on how much research you did, you will never write a paper that will get an A until you learn better research methods.

Poor Performance Produces Procrastination

One of the major reasons for procrastination is that people avoid activities in those areas where they have performed poorly in the past. Instead of setting a goal and making a plan to improve in a particular area, most people avoid that area altogether, which just makes the situation worse.

The reverse of this is that the *better* you become in a particular skill area, the more motivated you will be to perform that function, the less you will procrastinate, and the more determined you will be to get the job finished.

The fact is that everybody has both strengths and weaknesses. Refuse to rationalize, justify, or defend your areas of weakness. Instead, identify them clearly. Set a goal and make a plan to become very good in each of those areas. Just think! You may be only one critical skill away from top performance in your classes.

The Great Question

Here is one of the greatest questions you will ever ask and answer. "What one skill, if I developed and did it in an excellent fashion, would have the greatest positive impact on my school performance?"

You should use this question to guide your actions for the rest of your academic life. Look into yourself for the answer. You probably know what it is.

Ask your teachers this question. Ask your advisor or counselor. Ask your friends and your family. Whatever the answer is, go to work to bring up your performance in this area. Once you have asked, answered, and improved in one area, ask yourself the question again to improve in another key result area.

The good news is that all the skills you need to succeed at school are learnable. If others are excellent in that particular key result area, you might be discouraged and wonder why they are so good at it and you are not. To the contrary, this is a good thing! In reality, it is proof that you can become excellent as well if you decide to.

One of the best ways to stop procrastinating and get more things done faster is for you to become absolutely excellent in your key result areas. This can be as important as anything else you do in your life, school, and your future career.

Leverage Metacognition to Improve Your Skills

A powerful learning tool that you should develop is your sense of constantly assessing how much you know. This is called "metacognition," which literally means "understanding of what there is to understand."

The most exciting thing about metacognition is that it eliminates failure completely. When you ask yourself, "What do I know? What do I *not* know?" Your answer should include "Well, I don't know that *yet*." It doesn't matter if you know something or don't know it when you ask yourself these questions—the only issue is that you don't know it *yet*. In asking yourself these questions, you are giving yourself the opportunity to identify what you need to find out.

When you are studying for a test, review your notes in the following manner[1]:

- First identify everything you think you know.

- Then identify everything you don't know.

- Next, go through the things you *don't know* and look them all up and make a new study guide for yourself that includes those terms or concepts.

- Finally, double-check that you were right about the things you decided that you did know or understand. If you were mistaken about anything, add that to your study guide.

This simple four-step process can make your studying more effective by a whole letter grade!

There is an amazing phenomenon, originally named by researcher Janet Metcalfe, called the "hypercorrection effect."[2] Metcalfe's research demonstrates that when you get something wrong and then correct yourself, you will actually learn it much more effectively than if you had never been mistaken about it.

Every mistake is an opportunity—seize these opportunities to learn more and better.

EAT THAT FROG!

1. Identify the key result areas of your most important school project. What are they? Write down the key results you have to get to do the assignment in an excellent fashion. Give yourself a grade from one to ten on each one. And then determine the one key skill that, if you did it in an excellent manner, would help you the most in all your classes.

2. Take this list to your teacher or advisor and discuss it with him or her. Invite honest feedback and appraisal. You can only get better when you are open to the constructive input of other people. Discuss your conclusions with your parents or peers.

3. Always study for tests using the four-step metacognition process. It is important to identify what you don't know and to double-check that you are right about what you *think* you know.

   Make a habit of doing this analysis regularly, every term. Never stop improving. This decision alone can change your life.

PART FIVE

Proactively Dealing with Stress and What Causes It

Along with the pressure to achieve comes the stress you will feel as you work toward your goals. It is critically important that you learn how to proactively handle your stress. Throughout your life, you will face many stressful situations, and learning how to manage stress will be a huge key to your future success.

This part of the book is not about mindfulness, meditation, or self-care. These things are important, and if they work for you, then definitely continue using them. However, the most important tools I can give you to combat stress are preventative. If you take proactive steps to combat your stress before it becomes debilitating, you will have much more control over how stress impacts you later.

Planning ahead and preparing are two of the most powerful strategies to combat stress and anxiety. Intentionally managing your use of technology is another. Rather than offering damage control or band-aids, this section gives you preventative tools and guidance that will help you to manage your stress so that it doesn't overwhelm you in the first place!

18

Prepare Thoroughly before You Begin

No matter what the level of your ability, you have more potential than you can ever develop in a lifetime.

JAMES T. MCCAY

One of the best ways for you to overcome procrastination and stress is to have everything you need at hand before you begin. When you are fully prepared, you are like an archer with an arrow pulled back taut in the bow. You will be amazed at what you achieve in the months and years ahead. You just need one small mental push to get started.

Proper preparation is like getting everything ready to prepare a complete meal. You set all the ingredients out on the counter in front of you and then begin putting the meal together, one step at a time.

Begin by clearing off your desk or workspace so that you have only one task in front of you. If necessary, put everything else on the floor or somewhere else in your room—as long as it is out of sight.

Gather all the information, the textbook, research, notes from class, or other materials that you will require to complete the job. Have them at hand so you can reach them without getting up or moving around. If some of these are digital, close down all computer programs that are not essential to your task and open only the documents or programs you need to do your assignment. Be sure that you have all the writing materials, login information, access codes, email addresses, and everything else you need to start working and continue working until the job is done.

Set up your work area so that it is comfortable, attractive, and conducive to working for long periods. Especially, make sure that you have a comfortable chair that supports your back and allows your feet to rest flat on the floor.

Optimize Your Workspace

The most productive people take the time to create a work area where they enjoy spending time. The cleaner and neater your work area is before you begin, the easier it will be for you to get started and keep going.

When everything is laid out neatly and in sequence, you will feel much more like getting on with the job. A clear, organized workspace will eliminate mental noise and nagging worries and will go a long way to reducing the stress you feel when trying to work on your assignments, musical instrument practice, or college or job applications.

It is amazing how many books never get written, how many degrees never get completed, how many life-changing tasks never get started because people fail to take the first step of preparing everything in advance.

Tackle Your Frog

Once you have completed your preparations, it is essential that you launch immediately toward your goals. Get started. Do the first thing, whatever it is.

My personal rule is "Get it 80 percent right and then correct it later." Run it up the flagpole and see if anyone salutes. Don't expect perfection the first time or even the first few times. Be prepared to fail over and over before you get it right.

One unfortunate consequence of learning in a high-stress environment is a tendency toward perfectionism. A very old saying is "perfection is the enemy of the good," which basically means that if you try to be perfect, you may never produce anything at all.

Preparation and planning are essential in combatting perfectionism: you do not want to turn in an assignment you think might not pass muster, and for a test you have only one chance to get it right. You need to build in time to do an assignment all the way through *imperfectly* and then go back and see how to improve it. Make sure to get it 80 percent done several days before the final assignment is due, or be able to answer 80 percent of the questions on your test study guide several days in advance. Then take those final days to refine and improve your work or studies until you know you have prepared enough to do well.

Wayne Gretzky, the great hockey player, once said, "You miss 100 percent of the shots you don't take." Once you have completed your preparations, have the courage to take the first action, and everything else will follow from that. The way you develop the courage you need is to *act as if* you already had the courage and behave accordingly.

Take the First Step

When you sit down with everything in front of you, ready to go, assume the body language of high performance. Sit up straight; sit forward and away from the back of the chair. Carry yourself as though you were an efficient, effective, high-performing personality. Then, pick up the first item and say to yourself, "Let's get to work!" and plunge in. And once you've started, keep going until the task is finished.

EAT THAT FROG!

1. Take a good look at your desk or study area. Ask yourself, "What kind of a person works in an environment like this?" The cleaner and neater your work environment, the more positive, productive, and confident you will feel.

2. Resolve today to clean up your desk completely so that you feel effective, efficient, and ready to get going each time you sit down to study.

19
Focus Your Attention

All of life is the study of attention;
where your attention goes, your life follows.
JIDDU KRISHNAMURTI

Focused attention is the key to high performance. The "attraction of distraction," the lure of electronic and other interruptions, leads to diffused attention, a wandering mind, a lack of focus, and, ultimately, underachievement and failure.

Current research proves that continuously responding and reacting to emails, telephone calls and texts, and chat messages has a negative effect on your brain, shortening your attention span and making it difficult, if not impossible, for you to complete the tasks upon which your future and your success depend.[1]

The Three Ds of New Habit Formation

You need three key qualities to develop the habits of focus and concentration, which are all learnable. They are decision, discipline, and determination.

First, make a *decision* to develop the habit of task completion. Second, *discipline* yourself to practice the principles you are about to learn over and over until they become automatic. And third, back everything you do with *determination* until the habit is locked in and becomes a permanent part of your personality.

Developing an Addiction

When you check your messages and texts first thing in the morning or when you respond to the bell or other sound that indicates an incoming message, your brain releases a tiny shot of dopamine. This shot gives you a pleasant buzz. It stimulates your curiosity and causes you to react and respond immediately. You instantly forget whatever else you were doing and turn your full attention to the new message.

Like the sound of bells ringing when you win while playing a slot machine, the sound of an email notification triggers the reaction of "What did I win?" You immediately stop your task to find out what your "prize" is. When you start your day with a few shots of dopamine triggered by the sound of your phone's notifications going off, you will find it extremely difficult to pay close attention to your important tasks for the rest of the day.

Try leaving your phone in a drawer in the kitchen before you go to bed for the evening. If you use your phone or a wearable device as an alarm clock, ignoring notifications will be very challenging. If you can, choose not to look at any notifications that may have piled up overnight when your alarm goes off. If resisting the temptation is too difficult, try an old-fashioned alarm clock! When you wake up, make sure to do a few activities before getting your device or looking at any notifications. The time it takes to get dressed, eat breakfast, brush your teeth, and get your things together for school first will give your brain a chance to wake up without developing a mini–dopamine addiction.

The Multitasking Illusion

Some people believe that they can engage in multitasking, going back and forth between emails and homework. But people can focus only on one thing at a time. What they are really doing is called "task shifting." They are shifting their attention back and forth, like swinging a searchlight from one object to another.

After an internet interruption, it takes about fifteen minutes for you to shift your total attention back to your task and continue working. This is precisely why so many people today are working harder and harder, shifting from email interruptions to work and back again, all day long, and getting less and less accomplished. They also make more mistakes.

If you grew up in a digital environment, you may be extremely adept at task switching and feel you can do it much more rapidly than others. This might be true. However, it still is not true multitasking, and you will be losing time with every switch, no matter how fast you are.

The Proven Solutions

Solutions to these problems are simple and are being adopted by the most productive people in almost every context. First, don't check your notifications in the morning and immediately trigger the all-day dopamine addiction. Leave your devices off.

Second, if you must check your email or messages for any reason, get in and out fast. Turn off the sound on your computer, and put your phone on "vibrate" or give it to a parent until you are finished with your homework. Stop the stimulations that trigger the flow of dopamine and lead to continuous interruptions.

Finally, resolve to check your phone only twice a day during the school day, at 11:00 a.m. and 3:00 p.m. or when your school schedule allows, and then turn it off again each time. If you don't need your phone for class, try to leave it in your locker, or at least turn it off and zip it into your schoolbag. If you use a wearable, minimize the notifications you allow it to send. If you are serious and committed to increasing your productivity, try using an analog watch. You will be amazed at how much clarity and focus you unlock with this one small change.

Whenever you are in class, follow the same protocol. Leave electronic devices off. You might take notes on your laptop or need your computer for class activities, but turn off all notifications and open only the programs you need for class. Pay 100 percent attention to your teacher and class discussion. Even a wearable device should be silenced or turned off in class.

Here is a secret you might not believe: it is incredibly obvious when students are using their computers for anything other than class. All those times you thought you were getting away with being on a Google Docs Chat for the whole lecture, your teacher could tell what you were really doing. If you don't believe me, take a look around at the other students in the class. Are they looking up at the board every few seconds? Are they typing notes and occasionally raising their hand to participate in class discussions?

Or are they staring, mesmerized, into their screen without typing notes at all or typing furiously without ever looking up to check in with the lesson?

Remember, computers have been around for a long time now, and people in their forties grew up taking laptops to class. The programs may have been different, but they were doing exactly the same things today's students do.

Once you look at other students in the class as if you were their teacher, you will probably realize how easy it is to tell what they are doing—even if you can't see their screens. The sad part about this is that students who do not pay attention in class are actually creating their own barriers. Class is effortless learning—someone else is literally doing all the work in telling you the things you need to know! All you have to do is think about what you are hearing and remember it later. Not paying attention in class is a massive wasted opportunity. To catch up and do well on your assignments and tests, you will have to study three times harder on your own.

Resolve now to take advantage of the massive opportunity you have to pay attention in class. Turn off your notifications, and even try taking notes by hand. Neuroscientists have shown that your brain retains and processes information much more effectively when you handwrite notes.[2]

Double Your Productivity

Here is a simple way to double your productivity. This will work best on weekends or in the evenings when you are working on your homework for large chunks of time. First, plan each day or scheduled block of homework time in advance, select your most important task, and then start on that task first thing, before you do anything else.

Second, commit to working nonstop for a specific amount of time with no diversion or distraction. Use a kitchen timer instead of your phone's timer to remove temptation. The easiest way is to start work for thirty minutes and then give yourself a five-minute break. Then start another thirty-minute period of work. After a few days or weeks, once you can do this easily, work your way up to sixty minutes with a ten-minute break. Ultimately, try to work for ninety minutes with a fifteen-minute break. No matter how you break up the time blocks, after a three-hour work period, you can then reward yourself with a shot of dopamine by checking your messages.

When you develop the habit of completing three hours of important work every time you sit down to do your homework, no matter what, you will both double your productivity and break yourself of the habit of checking your notifications all day long. You will regain full control of your life.

— EAT THAT FROG! —

1. Keep your goals of success and high productivity in mind. Before you do anything, ask yourself, "Is this helping me achieve one of my most important goals, or is this just a distraction?"

2. Refuse to become a slave to the bells and whistles that distract you from completing those tasks that can make a real difference in your life. Leave nonessential devices and apps off.

20
Technology Is a Terrible Master

There is more to life than just increasing its speed.
MOHANDAS GANDHI

Someday in the future, we've all been told, we will be running around in special clothing that communicates with our bodies and our environment, looking through lenses that digitally enhance the world. We may not be there yet, but it is true that technology is already so woven into our everyday lives that we live and breathe it constantly. The never-ending barrage of notifications and emails and the pressure to know exactly what is going on with all your friends every second of the day constitute an enormous source of stress in today's schools and colleges.

Even if you are able to resist the temptation to constantly look at your phone, you are likely doing a portion or even most of your schoolwork on a digital device of some kind. That device is almost certainly connected to the internet, and the internet desperately wants your attention. In fact, in the tech industry, companies do not refer to "market share" anymore. Market share is the percentage of existing customers who buy a company's products. Instead, they refer to something called "mind-share." What they mean by this is that they consider the *mind* of their consumer to be their market, and they are spending billions of dollars to control as much of your mind as possible.

Since this is the reality, how you choose to manage your use of technology is going to have an incredible impact on your productivity, your achievement, and your success both in school and later in your life.

You Have a Choice

The most important thing to remember about your relationship with the digital world is that you do still have a choice. It may not always feel like it, but you do. Even if digital tools make it exceptionally hard, there are always ways to be in control of your digital life. Remember, even where technology is concerned, you are responsible for your choices and actions.

For you to stay calm, clearheaded, and capable of performing at your best, choose to detach on a regular basis from technology. A researcher who asked a group of CEOs and entrepreneurs to unplug from technology found they had improved memory, deeper relationships, better sleep, and a greater likelihood of making life-transforming decisions.[1]

When people are too plugged in, communications technology quickly becomes a destructive addiction. If you are anything like the average teenager or young adult in America, you may be spending as much as six to nine hours in front of a screen every day.[2]

From now on, turn your phone off when you go to sleep, and don't turn it on in the morning until you are fully awake and have gotten dressed and eaten breakfast. You can even try waiting until you have left the house. Don't start the addictive dopamine cycle right away.

Manage Your Notifications

The first and most important step in managing your technology is turning off as many notifications on your phone and computer as possible. Every app must ask your permission to send you notifications. You can go into the settings in your phone and turn off an app's ability to send these to you.

Letting notifications take over is a double challenge: they try to get your attention in real time and will distract you from whatever task you are working on in the moment. Then, even when you manage to ignore them for a time, a large backlog of notifications can sneakily masquerade as a to-do list, making you feel as if you have to look through all of them! Make no mistake: your backlog of 300 notifications is not as important as the to-do lists you have learned to make in this book.

Choose which apps you allow to send you notifications very carefully. Select just a few and turn off notifications for all other apps on your phone. This alone will save you hours every day.

Don't Give In to Temptation

You may need a computer to do some of your assignments. Unfortunately, a computer is one of the most challenging environments for personal productivity. It is a machine that has been built specifically to do millions of tasks at a time. Here's the thing to remember: the computer is meant to do millions of tasks at a time, but the human being using the computer is not!

It is easy to keep a chat box (or ten) open or a video going in the background, and of course, those invasive notifications are everywhere on your computer too. As with your phone, websites need to ask your permission to send you notifications. Make it a practice today to always choose "no" or "block" when a website asks you for permission to send you notifications.

If you have to chat with classmates to work on a project, do so intentionally and set specific times for the conversations—-and do so only between bursts of sustained, focused work. While it might be tempting to leave your chat windows open all the time, constantly chatting with friends while you are trying to focus will result in massive lost time and retention. In other words, when you are chatting, you learn poorly and remember less, and any work takes three times as long! The next time you sit down to do your homework, disable all your chat functions and see how long your assignments take you. (Here's betting you finish in one-third the time!)

If you get your work done without distractions, you will have much more time to actually hang out with your friends and family. This holds true even if your friends live far away from you and you use digital tools to communicate. Regardless of how you spend time with loved ones, you will still be able to focus better on a video call or text-based conversation if all your schoolwork is finished.

Fight the FOMO

A journalist for *Fortune* magazine once wrote that when he arrived back at the office after a two-week European vacation, he had more than 700 emails waiting for him. He realized that it would take him a week to get through them all before starting on important projects.

For the first time in his career, he took a deep breath and punched the Delete All button, erasing those 700 emails forever. He then got busy with the projects that were really important to him and his company.

His explanation was simple: "I realized that, just because somebody sends me an email, it does not mean that they own a piece of my life." Although not many people would delete their entire in-box, you can definitely delete and ignore more emails than you do right now. Empower yourself to remove all emails that don't relate to important goals and relationships.

The fear of missing out that drives many people to obsessively connect to their devices is a real and pervasive facet of modern life. The anxiety it produces is powerful and seductive—if you had just seen that *one* notification, you might not have missed an important piece of news, an event you would have liked, or a friend's personal life announcement. Like most forms of anxiety, however, this is a lie that your brain is telling you.

The reality is that you can never keep up with all the things that are happening in the world. Even if you were to quit school and obsessively read every single notification that came through on every device you own, you still wouldn't find out everything that might impact your life. You will miss everything going on in front of you though!

Accept that you can never keep up with everything, and focus instead on what is in front of you. Try a new relationship with the digital world and see how much more time you have every day!

EAT THAT FROG!

1. Create zones of silence during your day-to-day activities. Turn off your computer and your phone (and any other digital devices) for one hour in the morning and one hour in the afternoon. You will be amazed at what happens: nothing.

2. Resolve to unplug from technology for one full day each week. By the end of your digital detox, your mind will be calm and clear. When your mental batteries have time to recharge, you will be much more effective at eating frogs. Plan this time with friends and family—instead of being stressed about what you might be missing online, engage with a group of people around you.

21

Technology Is a Wonderful Servant

Technology is just a tool.

MELINDA GATES

With technology's infinite attempts to command your attention, it is absolutely necessary that you learn to treat your digital tools as if you control them, rather than allowing them to control you. When you are successful in this, technology will make your life easier and smoother, not harder and more stressful.

Many learning tools are now digitally based, and you may even be required to use a digital tool to track your schedule, your assignments, or group projects. Productivity apps and learning tools can be powerful, but they are not a magic wand that will solve all your problems.

Imagine: it is a new school year and you are getting ready for the year ahead. You just heard about this amazing new scheduling app and you download it right away. You start out by setting it up, putting all your classes into it, and organizing them. It seems great! But then three weeks in, you lose track. You start forgetting to put assignments into the app, you hardly ever remember to look at it, and then three months into the school year you have forgotten you ever tried it. But there is this great new productivity app you just heard about and you think it is finally going to get you on track!

Sound familiar?

Don't get stuck on the merry-go-round of always trying the next app, thinking, "This is it! This is the one that is going to magically make me more productive!" only to completely forget about it a few weeks later.

You Must Be Strategic

App-based productivity tools are just like anything else— they are no better than writing your to-do list with pen and paper. Any tool is only as good as the use you make of it. Whether you choose to track your to-do lists and assignments digitally or on paper, the key is to be consistent.

When you try a new productivity app, make sure to stick with it for at least two months. Don't allow yourself to jump from app to app, never really benefiting from any of them. When you try one, commit to it and stick with it.

Once you have used the app consistently for a while, evaluate how much it is helping you. Is it easy to remember to put information and assignments in? Do you make it through your to-do lists? Have you noticed a difference in your stress levels or productivity since starting to use it?

If an app is working for you, keep using it! No matter how tempting the next tool might be, you are better off sticking with something that works rather than wasting time learning yet a new interface.

And just maybe, try managing your productivity with pen and paper to see how it stacks up. When you put a to-do list on your phone, you are not looking at it all the time. The minute you need to open a learning app or sign into your email, the to-do list disappears from your sight—and as they say, out of sight, out of mind.

Give a pen-and-paper tracking system a shot. You can keep your to-do list where you can see it at all times. While you are working on your computer, you can keep your assignments and day planner out on the desk beside you for easy reference. You may be surprised at how well an analog tracking system works for you.

Take Control of Your Communication

When you sit down to study on a computer, clear your digital workspace as you would your physical desk: close every program not needed for the task at hand. Block the websites that distract you the most. Make sure that only the communication channels you need to complete your task are open. Some tasks will require communication, but having ten different ways to communicate is over-kill. Once only relevant information is visible on your screen, arrange your windows for perfect workflow.

After your notification purge from the last chapter, you have only a few apps left with the ability to distract you from your task. However, when you are focusing on a major task, you should disable *all* notifications—both audio and visual—even from the apps that you still allow notifications from normally. This is an important step toward checking your phone on your own schedule and thus regaining control of your life. If you still have trouble resisting the temptation to open these programs, hide your phone, turn it all the way off, or give it to a parent.

But What about Emergencies?

You may feel that unplugging from technology or disabling notifications is simply not an option. Even as a teenager, you may have responsibilities for younger siblings, parents who expect to be able to reach you at all times, or friends who rely on you for emotional support.

This is an absolutely valid concern. The solution, however, is not to be available to everyone at all times. Rather, create a dedicated, emergencies-only phone number, email address, or other communication channel. For example, you can choose a specific chat app to use only to connect with people who might need to get in touch with you in an emergency situation.

This channel should be like your own personal 911. It is important to remember that this channel is meant only for extreme emergencies—such as when the physical or mental health of someone is in danger, a sibling is stranded at day care, or a parent needs to get in touch with you urgently. If close friends are in your emergency network, include only the most essential.

If you want, you can set up something similar for your academic life as well. Program your email in-box to automatically sort emails from your professors, teachers, or online learning platforms into a "Read First" folder.

In other words, segment your communication channels so that only frogs can hop into your castle of concentration.

The Land of Infinite Possibility

The amount of information that is available to us all at the touch of a screen is extraordinary. In a few seconds, it is possible to access a seemingly endless stream of resources. Research that would have taken your parents hours in a library, and that would have been limited by that library's collection, now can be done from your home in a fraction of the time.

However, it is also incredibly easy to accidentally plagiarize in this world of infinite data. Plagiarism is not always copying text verbatim. (Though you shouldn't do that either! Be assured—your teacher has also googled "9th grade essay about the green light at the end of the pier Great Gatsby" and knows all the prepackaged essays that are available.) You may be required to use a program like Turnitin or Grammarly to check for any plagarized content.

Plagiarism includes using ideas directly from an external source without crediting them. Here are some examples:

- Paraphrasing a source by changing the specific wording but copying the main idea
- Using the argument from a source as your own thesis

- Referencing an idea from a source in your paper without claiming it as your own but neglecting to cite the source properly
- Writing a paper with the same basic argument structure as a source, even if you use different examples and write it in your own words

Make sure to write down your sources as you are doing your research! The best way to manage sources is to write down every one you read right away, no matter whether you have started writing your paper or not. There is no bigger waste of time than going back to figure out which of your sources you remember using. Make your bibliography as you go; don't try to reengineer it at the end of a project.

Own Your Learning—the Sky's the Limit

Beyond infinite information, the internet also allows you unprecedented access to experts. When in history have people been able to look up and find the contact information for Nobel laureates, college professors, or famous writers? Reaching out to experts can be a powerful way to take control of your own learning.

If you are working on a project and discover people who are doing research on that topic, it is often possible for you to reach out directly with questions. They may not always write back, but they might if you write a short, respectful, and specific email with your questions.

In addition to experts, there are also many different learning tools that may offer you new ways of learning and interacting with the subjects you are studying in school. Having trouble with math? You can search for the topic that is giving you trouble on Khan Academy. YouTube offers millions of learning videos that cover almost everything you would learn in a standard high school curriculum. You can augment what you are learning in your own school with information from many different sources.

The internet also offers access to learning tools that might offer you a better fit for your particular learning style. If you are struggling with schoolwork and don't seem to be getting the support you need from your school, you can seek out support online. Students LEAD is one such resource. You can sign on and use its tools to assess your learning style. The website will then offer you specific tactics for studying and learning based on your individual strengths and weaknesses.

You can find more information about Khan Academy and Students LEAD in the "Learning Resources" section.

Learning is more in your own control than ever before in history—largely due to the internet. The trick is to take full advantage of everything technology offers you without letting it become the master of your time. You are the one responsible for your time—you get to choose. Choose to treat technology like a useful tool and you will be well on your way to enormous success!

EAT THAT FROG!

1. Turn off all notifications, except for your emergency channels. Create special areas in your digital life for your most important tasks.

2. Resolve to try out any new app that will help you be more efficient and focused for at least two months before jumping ship and trying the next new thing.

3. In addition to what you were assigned by your teacher, seek out resources that will help you learn more and learn better online.

22
Practice Creative Procrastination

Make time for getting big tasks done every day.
Plan your daily workload in advance. Single out the
relatively few small jobs that absolutely must be
done immediately in the morning. Then go directly
to the big tasks and pursue them to completion.
BOARDROOM REPORTS

Creative procrastination is one of the most effective of all personal performance techniques. It can change your life. Yes, you read that right. Procrastination, when intentionally employed, can be a good strategy!

The fact is that you can't do everything that you have to do. You have to procrastinate on something. Therefore, deliberately and consciously procrastinate on small tasks. Put off eating smaller or less ugly frogs. Eat the biggest and ugliest frogs before anything else. Do the worst first!

Here is a secret: everyone procrastinates. The difference between high performers and low performers is largely determined by *what they choose to procrastinate on*.

Since you must procrastinate anyway, decide today to procrastinate on low-value activities. Decide to procrastinate on or eliminate those activities that don't make much of a contribution to your life in any case. Get rid of the tadpoles and focus on the frogs.

Priorities versus Posteriorities

Here is a key point. To set proper priorities, you must set posteriorities as well. A *priority* is something that you do more of and sooner, while a *posteriority* is something that you do less of and later, if at all.

> **Rule:** You can get your time and your life under control only to the degree to which you discontinue lower-value activities.

One of the most powerful of all words in time management is *no!* Say it politely. Say it clearly so that there are no misunderstandings. Say it regularly as a normal part of your time management vocabulary. You may not be able to say no to a school assignment, but there are many things in your life that you can say no to. If someone asks you to join yet another club after school, you can say no. You can say no to social activities—especially if they are not something you would actually enjoy but might feel peer pressure to participate in.

Warren Buffett, one of the richest men in the world, was once asked his secret of success. He replied, "Simple. I just say no to everything that is not absolutely vital to me at the moment."

Say no to anything that is not a high-value use of your time and your life. Say no gently but firmly to avoid agreeing to something you really don't think is in your best interests. Say it early and say it often. Remember that you have no spare time; there is only time and what you choose to do with it.

For you to do something new, you must complete or stop doing something old. This is called "opportunity cost": the cost of doing something is *not* doing something else. Picking up means putting down.

Creative procrastination is the act of thoughtfully and deliberately deciding upon the exact things you are not going to do right now, if ever.

Procrastinate on Purpose

Most people engage in *unconscious* procrastination. They procrastinate without thinking about it. As a result, they procrastinate on the big, valuable, important tasks that can have significant long-term consequences. You must avoid this common tendency at all costs.

Your job is to deliberately procrastinate on tasks that are of low value so that you have more time for tasks that can make a big difference in your life and schoolwork. Continually review your obligations and activities to identify time-consuming, low-value tasks that you can abandon with no real loss. This should be an ongoing practice for you that never ends.

Begin today to practice creative procrastination. Set posteriorities wherever and whenever you can. This decision alone can enable you to get your time and your life under control.

EAT THAT FROG!

1. Practice "zero-based thinking" in every part of your life. Ask yourself continually, "If I were not doing this already, knowing what I now know, would I start doing it again today?" If it is something you would not start again today, knowing what you now know, it is a prime candidate for abandonment or creative procrastination.

2. Examine each of your school and extracurricular activities and evaluate it based on your current situation. Select at least one activity to abandon immediately or at least deliberately put off until your more important goals have been achieved.

Conclusion

Putting It All Together

The key to happiness, satisfaction, great success, and a wonderful feeling of personal power and effectiveness is for you to develop the habit of eating your frog first thing every day. Fortunately, this is a learnable skill that you can acquire through repetition. And when you develop the habit of starting on your most important task before anything else, your success is assured.

Here is a summary of all the concrete tools this book presented to help you stop procrastinating and get more things done faster. Review these rules and principles regularly until they become firmly ingrained in your thinking and actions, and your future will be guaranteed.

1. **Self-esteem:** First, set out to conquer your fears. Next, identify and then live your values every day. Finally, challenge yourself to leave your comfort zone.

2. **Personal responsibility:** Always remember that you are 100 percent responsible for every action

you take. You can't control others' actions or per-
ceptions, but you can always control your own
reactions.

3. **Goals:** Nothing is more powerful than clear, written goals. Always write your goals down using the
Three P Formula rather than keeping them inside
your head. Always specify a reasonable timeframe
for achieving your goals.

4. **Set the table:** Decide exactly what you want.
Clarity is essential. Write out your goals and objectives before you begin.

5. **Plan every day in advance:** Think on paper.
Every minute you spend in planning can save you
five or ten minutes in execution.

6. **Study strategically using long and short
chunks of time:** Choose what to study based on
how long you have: choose memory tasks for study
hall and work on big papers when you have large
blocks of time so you can concentrate for extended
periods.

7. **Apply the 80/20 Rule to everything:** Twenty
percent of your activities will account for 80 percent
of your results. Always concentrate your efforts on
that top 20 percent.

8. **Slice and dice the task:** Break large, complex
tasks down into bite-sized pieces, and then do just
one small part of the task to get started.

9. **Consider the consequences:** Your most important tasks and priorities are those that can have the most serious consequences, positive or negative, on your life or schoolwork. Focus on these above all else.

10. **Take it one mile marker at a time:** Even if you don't yet know how you will complete 100 percent of a task, you can always take at least one action that moves the task forward.

11. **Motivate yourself into action:** Be your own cheerleader. Look for the good in every situation. Focus on the solution rather than the problem. Always be optimistic and constructive.

12. **Single handle every task:** Set clear priorities, start immediately on your most important task, and then work without stopping until the job is 100 percent complete. This is the real key to high performance and maximum personal productivity.

13. **Develop a sense of urgency:** Make a habit of moving fast on your key tasks. Become known as a person who does things quickly and well.

14. **Put the pressure on yourself:** Imagine that you have to leave town for a month, and work as if you had to get your major task completed before you left.

15. **Learn how to learn:** The better you are at learning itself, the faster you will be able to learn all the material you need to for class. The more knowledgeable

and skilled you become at your key skills, the faster you start them and the sooner you get them done. Determine exactly what it is that you are very good at doing, or could be very good at, and throw your whole heart into doing those specific things very, very well.

16. **Identify your key constraints:** Determine the bottlenecks or choke points, internal or external, that set the speed at which you achieve your most important goals, and focus on alleviating them.

17. **Focus on key result areas:** Identify those results that you absolutely, positively have to get to be successful, and work on them all day long.

18. **Prepare thoroughly before you begin:** Have everything you need at hand before you start. Assemble all the papers, information, tools, work materials, and logins you might require so that you can get started and keep going.

19. **Focus your attention:** Stop the interruptions and distractions that interfere with completing your most important tasks.

20. **Technology is a terrible master:** Take back your time from enslaving technological addictions. Learn to often turn devices off and leave them off.

21. **Technology is a wonderful servant:** Use your technological tools to confront yourself with what is most important and protect yourself from what is least important.

22. **Practice creative procrastination:** Since you can't do everything, you must learn to deliberately put off those tasks that are of low value so that you have enough time to do the few things that really count.

Make a decision to practice these principles every day until they become second nature to you. With these habits of personal management as a permanent part of your personality, your future success will be unlimited.

Just do it! *Eat that frog!*

Notes

Chapter 9

1. Andrew Blackman, "The Inner Workings of the Executive Brain," *Wall Street Journal*, April 27, 2014.

Chapter 15

1. Pooja K. Agarwal and Patrice M. Bain, *Powerful Teaching: Unleash the Science of Learning* (San Francisco: Jossey-Bass, 2019).

Chapter 17

1. Powerful Teaching, "Four Steps of Metacognition," 2019, https://www.powerfulteaching.org/resources.
2. John Dunlosky and Janet Metcalfe, *Metacognition* (Thousand Oaks, CA: Sage Publications, 2009).

Chapter 19

1. Leon Watson, "Humans Have Shorter Attention Span Than Goldfish, Thanks to Smartphones," *Telegraph*, May 15, 2015, http://www.telegraph.co.uk/science/2016/03/12/humans-have-shorter-attention-span-than-goldfish-thanks-to-smart/.

2. Pam A. Mueller and Daniel M. Oppenheimer, "The Pen Is Mightier Than the Keyboard: Advantages of Longhand over Laptop Note Taking," *Psychological Science*, 25 no. 6 (April 2014): 1159–1168, https://doi.org/10.1177/0956797614524581.

Chapter 20

1. Elizabeth Segran, "What Really Happens to Your Brain and Body during a Digital Detox," *Fast Company*, July 30, 2015, http://www.fastcompany.com/3049138/most-creative-people/what-really-happens-to-your-brain-and-body-during-a-digital-detox.

2. Victoria Rideout and Michael B. Robb, *The Common Sense Census: Media Use by Tweens and Teens* (San Francisco: Common Sense Media, 2019), https://www.commonsensemedia.org/sites/default/files/uploads/research/2019-census-8-to-18-full-report-updated.pdf.

Learning Resources

Now that you have read this book, I hope you have been inspired to take control of your own learning. The following books and online tools are just a fraction of the resources that exist, but these tools can get you started.

Online Tools

Khan Academy, https://www.khanacademy.org/. Now a household name, Khan Academy might already be integrated into your school curriculum. However, you can use it on your own. If you are having trouble with a topic or skill and you want to seek out a different viewpoint or method of teaching, Khan Academy is the place to go.

Coursera, https://www.coursera.org/. Coursera is another online learning platform with courses on an enormous range of topics. This website includes courses that go beyond K–12 academics; it includes business skills and has a particular strength in courses in computer science and coding languages. It is not 100 percent free, but many of its resources are. Make sure your search terms are very specific on this website!

Online University Lecture Courses. Many of the world's top research institutions have been making some full university courses available online for years. These schools include Harvard University, Yale University, Massachusetts Institute of Technology, Princeton University, Stanford University, the University of California, Berkeley, the University of Arizona, Sapienza University of Rome, the University of Pennsylvania, the Ohio State University, Oxford University, Universidad Carlos III de Madrid—the list is almost endless. A Google search for online university courses will lead you to many web pages with lists of available courses. These are completely free and will give you access to some of the most cutting-edge scholarship in the world. Don't be intimidated by the college level—you won't be tested or assessed on what you learn! You can just listen to the videos and learn what the professor has to offer.

If you watch a series of lectures and deeply engage with the content, you may want to see if you can find the professor's email listed on the university or departmental website. A short, respectful email with a question about something from the lecture may even result in a valuable opportunity to learn even more if the professor is able to respond. (But don't be offended if you do not get a reply. Professors are extremely overworked and often are not able to respond to every email they receive.)

Students LEAD, Friday Institute for Innovative Education, https://studentslead.fi.ncsu.edu. If you have ever been frustrated with yourself and wondered why you were putting in enormous amounts of time and effort and still not succeeding, you might want to check this site out. Different people learn in different ways, and the assessment offered will help you learn about yourself and the way you take in and process information. The tools and resources are completely free! You can use what you learn from LEAD and apply it to your own studying, or you can reach out to your teachers and share your results—they may be able to teach you more effectively if they know.

Books on Learning

Check out your school and local library for any of these books on learning. Not only can you learn material better, but you can teach yourself how to be better at learning itself! Some of these books are written for students, and some are written for teachers. Although you are a student, all of these books can be valuable to you—you can still learn the techniques.

How We Learn: The Surprising Truth about When, Where, and Why It Happens by Benedict Carey

Learning How to Learn: How to Succeed in School without Spending All Your Time Studying; A Guide for Kids and Teens by Barbara Oakley and Terrence Sejnowski, with Alistair McConville

Make It Stick: The Science of Successful Learning by Peter C. Brown, Henry L. Roediger III, and Mark A. McDaniel

Mindshift: Break through Obstacles to Learning and Discover Your Hidden Potential by Barbara Oakley

Powerful Teaching: Unleash the Science of Learning by Pooja K. Agarwal and Patrice M. Bain

Understanding How We Learn: A Visual Guide by Yana Weinstein and Megan Sumeracki, with Oliver Caviglioli

Brian Tracy's Online Training Programs: The Key to Ultimate Success in Any Area of Your Life

TIME MANAGEMENT FOR RESULTS

If you enjoyed the timeless lessons in *Eat That Frog! for Students*, be sure to check out Time Management for Results, Brian Tracy's online training course for time management mastery. This course is designed for those who want to learn, develop, or improve their time management skill set so they can maximize their productivity and achieve greater success in every aspect of life.

To learn more about Time Management for Results, visit https://www.briantracy.com/catalog/time-management-for-results.

GOALS QUICKSTART MASTERCLASS

If you're looking to make true change in your life, check out the Goals Quickstart Masterclass. When you set a goal through Brian Tracy's new, transformational program, you'll be able to confidently move forward knowing you have a plan in place that will quickly drive you toward success. This program provides you with the clarity and confidence you need to dissolve self-imposed limitations and become an unequivocal powerhouse in the pursuit of your biggest, most important dreams.

To learn more about the Goals Quickstart Masterclass, visit https://www.briantracy.com/success/sp/goals/goals-quickstart-masterclass.html.

About the Authors

Brian Tracy is one of the top business speakers in the world today. He has designed and presented seminars for more than 1,000 large companies and more than 10,000 small and medium-sized enterprises in seventy-five countries on the subjects of leadership, management, professional selling, business model reinvention, and profit improvement. He has addressed more than 5,000,000 people in more than 5,000 talks and presentations worldwide. He currently speaks to 250,000 people per year. His fast-moving, entertaining digital training programs are taught in thirty-eight countries.

Brian is a bestselling author. He has written more than eighty books that have been translated into forty-two languages, including *Kiss That Frog!*, *Find Your Balance Point*, *Goals!*, *Flight Plan*, *Maximum Achievement*, *No Excuses!*, *Advanced Selling Strategies*, and *How the Best Leaders Lead*. He is happily married, with four children and five grandchildren. He is the president of Brian Tracy International and lives in Solana Beach, California. He can be reached at briantracy@briantracy.com.

Anna Leinberger is a writer, editor, and former educator. In addition to the occasional ghostwriting project, she acquires and edits books on women's leadership and empowerment, communication, intersectional feminism, nonviolence, the Middle East, and nontraditional leadership methodologies. Her authors include award-winning peacemakers, counterterrorism experts, tech executives, and *New York Times* bestselling authors.

She started her career as a teaching fellow at Kings Academy, the first boarding school in the Middle East, in Madaba, Jordan. She subsequently taught writing in Argentina, and she earned her California teaching credential while teaching for Kaplan International before switching to a career in book editing.

Outside of work, she serves on the board of the Metta Center for Nonviolence, sails in the windy San Francisco Bay, and travels as much as possible. She is married to a nautical archaeologist and lives in Berkeley, California, with her extremely smug cat, Fey.

Also by Brian Tracy

Eat That Frog! Third Edition

21 Great Ways to Stop Procrastinating and Get More Done in Less Time

There's an old saying that if the first thing you do each morning is eat a live frog, you'll have the satisfaction of knowing you're done with the worst thing you'll have to do all day. For Tracy, "eating a frog" is a metaphor for tackling your most challenging task—but also the one that can have the greatest positive impact on your life. *Eat That Frog!* shows you how to organize each day so you can zero in on these critical tasks and accomplish them efficiently and effectively. In this fully revised and updated edition, Tracy adds two new chapters. The first explains how you can use technology to remind yourself of what is most important and protect yourself from what is least important. The second offers advice for maintaining focus in our era of constant distractions, electronic and otherwise.

Paperback, ISBN 978-1-62656-941-6
PDF ebook, ISBN 978-1-62656-942-3
ePub ebook, ISBN 978-1-62656-943-0
Digital audio, ISBN 978-1-62656-944-7

BK· Berrett–Koehler Publishers, Inc.
www.bkconnection.com   800.929.2929

Also by Brian Tracy

Eat That Frog! Action Workbook

21 Great Ways to Stop Procrastinating and Get More Done in Less Time

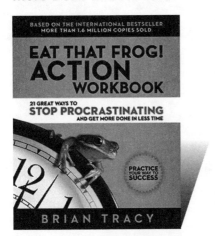

Based on Brian Tracy's *Eat That Frog!*—a modern classic that's been translated into over forty languages—this workbook can be used on its own or along with the book. There are exercises that correspond to each chapter. "Eating a frog" is a metaphor for tackling your most challenging—but most valuable—task first. This workbook is designed to help you do just that. Packed full of exercises, assessments, tips, and tools, it shows how to organize your day so you can zero in on these critical tasks and accomplish them efficiently and effectively. The *Eat That Frog! Action Workbook* will help you achieve your most important goals faster than you ever thought possible!

Paperback, ISBN 978-1-5230-8470-8
PDF ebook, ISBN 978-1-5230-9393-9
ePub ebook, ISBN 978-1-5230-9537-7

Berrett–Koehler Publishers, Inc.
www.bkconnection.com   **800.929.2929**

Also by Brian Tracy

Eat That Frog! Cards
Stop Procrastinating and Get More Done in Less Time

Designed for individual or group play, these cards offer a fun, hands-on way to identify what's holding you back and develop the right strategies to stop procrastinating and get more done. One set of cards in the deck describes procrastination habits, which you rank in order of importance. Do you become paralyzed by the length of your to-do list? Do you work on simple but low impact tasks first and neglect the harder, higher-impact tasks? Are you too easily distracted by social media? Once you've ranked your negative habits, you then match these "problem" cards with "solution" cards that describe strategies for overcoming them. You'll end up with a comprehensive, memorable, and personalized guide to dealing with your biggest behavioral obstacles to success.

Card deck, 56 cards, ISBN 978-1-5230-8469-2

Berrett–Koehler Publishers, Inc.
www.bkconnection.com   800.929.2929

Dear reader,

Thank you for picking up this book and welcome to the worldwide BK community! You're joining a special group of people who have come together to create positive change in their lives, organizations, and communities.

What's BK all about?

Our mission is to connect people and ideas to create a world that works for all.

Why? Our communities, organizations, and lives get bogged down by old paradigms of self-interest, exclusion, hierarchy, and privilege. But we believe that can change. That's why we seek the leading experts on these challenges—and share their actionable ideas with you.

A welcome gift

To help you get started, we'd like to offer you a **free copy** of one of our bestselling ebooks:

www.bkconnection.com/welcome

When you claim your **free ebook**, you'll also be subscribed to our blog.

Our freshest insights

Access the best new tools and ideas for leaders at all levels on our blog at ideas.bkconnection.com.

Sincerely,

Your friends at Berrett-Koehler

Certified

Corporation